SAVE OREGON
An Environmental Resource Directory

SAVE OREGON
An Environmental Resource Directory

Ann Brandvig and Richard Becker

CHRONICLE BOOKS • SAN FRANCISCO

Copyright © 1991 by Ann Brandvig and Richard Becker

All rights reserved. No part of this book may be reproduced without written permission from the publisher.

Printed in the United States of America

Library of Congress Cataloging-in-Publication Data
Brandvig, Ann.
  Save Oregon : an environmental resource directory / Ann Brandvig, Richard Becker.
     p. cm.
   ISBN 0-8118-0009-1 (pbk.)
   1. Environmental protection—Oregon—Citizen participation.
2. Environmental protection—Oregon—Directories. 3. Environmental protection—Oregon—Citizen participation—Information services—Directories. I. Becker, Richard. II. Title
TD171.7.B73 1991
363.7'07'09795—dc20   91-12046
                                                            CIP

10 9 8 7 6 5 4 3 2 1

Chronicle Books
275 Fifth Street
San Francisco, CA 94103

*Our legacy to our children
Aaron, Amanda, Isaac, and Jerrell:
a cleaner Earth*

Contents..............................

HOW TO MAKE A START   1

HOW TO USE THIS DIRECTORY   4

PART I: STEPS TO SAVING OREGON

    ENERGY CONSERVATION   6

    RECYCLING   13

    WATER POLLUTION   15

    WATER CONSERVATION   18

    CLEAN AIR AND TRANSPORTATION   22

    ENVIRONMENTALLY SMART PRODUCTS   26

    THE SAFEST FOOD: ORGANIC AND TRANSITIONAL   32

    GARDENS: GROWING ORGANIC   34

    SOCIALLY RESPONSIBLE INVESTING   38

    GETTING INVOLVED   40

PART II: OUTLETS AND SOURCES

    AUTOMOBILE PRODUCTS
        Antifreeze   44
        Smog Reduction   44

    AUTOMOBILES AND SCOOTERS, ENERGY EFFICIENT   45

BAGS
    Cotton Shopping Bags 46
    Paper Trash Bags 52
    Sandwich-Bag Substitutes 53

BATTERIES
    Code Red Batteries 53
    Rechargeable Batteries 54

CLEANING SUPPLIES 56

COMPOSTING
    Bins 65
    Information 69
    Supplies 70

DIAPERS
    Biodegradable Paper Diapers 72
    Cotton Diapers 73
    Diaper Services 74

ELECTED OFFICIALS TO LOBBY
    Politicians at the State Level 74
    Oregon Politicians at the National Level 75

ENERGY EXTENSION SERVICE, OREGON STATE UNIVERSITY 76

ENVIRONMENTAL ACTION GROUPS 77

ENVIRONMENTAL EDUCATION TOOLS AND SOURCES 86

●●●●●●●●●●●●●●●●●●●●●●●●●●●●●●●●●

FOOD, ORGANIC
    Baby Food 88
    Farmers' Markets 93
    Produce 95

GARDEN AND LAWN CARE, ORGANIC 104

INSULATION
    Drapes as Insulation 105
    Glass as Insulation 108
    Weatherstripping 108
    Window Films and Tinting 108

INVESTMENTS, SOCIALLY RESPONSIBLE
    Credit Cards 109
    Financial Advisors 110
    Information 112
    Local Capital Resources 113
    Local Investments 115
    Long-Distance Telephone Plans 115
    Money-Market Funds 115
    Mutual Funds 116
    Professional Groups 118

LIGHT BULBS, COMPACT FLUORESCENT 118

NATIVE OREGON PLANTS
    Information Sources and Plant Societies 121
    Plant Sources 122

NURSERIES, ORGANIC PLANT   124

PAINTS AND STAINS, NONTOXIC   127

PAPER, RECYCLED
    Bond, Computer, Writing, and Xerographic Papers   129
    Industrial Paper   134
    Paper Mills   134
    Toilet Paper, Paper Towels, and Facial Tissues   136

PEST CONTROL, SAFE
    Beneficial Organisms   143
    Exterminators   148
    Pesticides and Insecticides   151

POLLUTION COMPLAINTS   155
    DEQ Regional Offices   157

PRINTERS USING RECYCLED PAPER   158

PUBLICATIONS
    Energy Conservation and Alternative Sources   158
    Gardening   160
    Issues and Groups   162
    Life Style   165
    Political Resources   165
    Recycling   165
    Safe-Products Catalogs   167
    Safe-Products Guides   168
    Socially Responsible Investments   169

PUBLIC TRANSPORTATION 170

RECYCLED PRODUCTS ON THE MARKET
- Beer in Recycled Bottles 175
- Building Materials 175
- Bumpers, Protective 176
- Concrete Chunks 176
- Envirotek Products 177
- Floor Mats 177
- Foundation Vents 177
- Insulation, Cellulose 178
- Logs, Compressed Wood 178
- Oil, Rerefined Lubricating 179
- Paper Bags for Groceries 179
- Sewage Sludge 180
- Speed Bumps 180
- Stained Glass 181
- Topsoil 181

RECYCLING 181
- Batteries 182
- Contact People 182
- Hazardous Waste 189
- Paper Products, Glass, Metal, Oil, and Plastic 190
- Recycling by Businesses In-house 196
- Tires 198
- Yard Debris 198

SEEDS, ORGANIC 202

SHOWER HEADS, LOW-FLOW 207

SOIL AMENDMENTS, ORGANIC 208

SOLAR ENERGY
- Information 218
- Photovoltaics 220
- Solar Hot Water and Space Heating 223
- Tax Credits and Loans 227

WATER CONSERVATION PRODUCTS
- Car Wash Additive 228
- Soil Moisture Retainer 228
- Watering Systems and Water Timers 229
- Water Restrictors and a Recycler 233

WATER PURIFIERS AND FILTERS 234

WEATHERIZATION
- Free Energy Audits 235
- Tax Credits, Rebates, and Low-Interest Loans 236

WIND POWER
- Consultants 238
- Wind Electric System Dealers 238
- Water Pumping Windmill Dealers 239

FORM FOR FUTURE DIRECTORIES 241

How to Make a Start

> *This we know, that the Earth does not belong to man; man belongs to the Earth.... Man did not weave the web of life, he is merely a strand in it. Whatever he does to the web, he does to himself.*
>
> **CHIEF SEATTLE, SUQUAMISH, 1853**

The products we buy and how we use them affect our neighbors, our children, our planet. Buy bleached paper and dioxins flow into the Columbia River. Pour a quart of used motor oil down your drain and you contaminate 250,000 gallons of water. Take a ten-minute drink from a Styrofoam cup and you have squandered landfill space for five hundred years.

We all feel overwhelmed with the number of products and practices that foul our earth. Many of these practices continue because people don't know who stocks unbleached paper, where to recycle hazardous waste, or that the life expectancy of the little Styrofoam cup is so long.

This guide explains how to reshape life styles and offers the easiest ways to make the changes entailed. If you knew where to call for a free energy audit you could enjoy a cheaper, warmer winter, while minimizing your contribution to the greenhouse effect. If you could name the gizmo that decreases your faucet's water flow (a restrictor) and knew where to ask for it, you could save hundreds of gallons of water each week.

For decades we were told that technology would save us, that we could consume without worry. Technology cannot save us. We are running out of resources. Each day the air becomes dirtier, the water more poisonous, and the soil more chemically polluted. Each day we do nothing the problem grows. We cannot wait for someone else to solve our problems. We must take action now. Time is short.

The 1990s will be a crucial decade for this planet we call home. The bill for decades of unrestrained consumption has come due and we have no choice. We owe it to our children. It is time to reduce, recycle, and reuse.

While compiling this book, we made hundreds of phone calls to discover where Oregonians could find everything from environmental action groups to organic vegetable starts. As we searched for safe products and services, we asked a lot of questions, and sought out caring, ethical people. When we believed an individual or store was jumping on the green bandwagon for a fast green buck, we chose others who seemed honestly concerned about environment first, profit second.

Many new, environmental strategies for consumption are imperfect solutions. Yes, we need to recycle plastic, but unless we also buy floor mats and picnic tables made from recycled plastic we'll always have trouble finding recycling depots for that old shampoo jug. The solutions in this directory are just the beginning; they allow us to take action today, in our homes and in our lives.

> *We never thought Americans would have to choose. For the first time we are beginning to realize that we can't have everything. The price of the future, then, will be found in the things we give up.*
>
> **INDUSTRIALIST IRWIN MILLER**

Turning off the water while brushing our teeth is easy. Such other steps as composting, recycling, and using public transit take more time and thought. We all have wasteful habits. Adjustment time is necessary before these changes feel comfortable. It was several months before we ourselves reliably remembered to bring our canvas shopping bag to the market. Occasionally we forget, but we're doing better.

With this directory you'll find the best environmental products to date. Ask your neighborhood stores to carry them. We spoke with many retail store managers, and they told us, "When people request it, we stock it." If only 10 percent of all customers made these requests, merchants would pay attention.

When we ask for stationery printed on recycled paper, printers will carry it. (Under Paper, Recycled, we give you the names of retail suppliers and of distributors from whom your printer can order it.) When we buy nontoxic pesticides, garden stores will provide more organic choices. (We list brands, garden shops with an organic emphasis, and catalogs that sell only nontoxic pesticides, fungicides, and fertilizers.) When we demand shopping bags of recycled paper instead of plastic, plastic bags will disappear. (We list manufacturers of recycled bags, and stores that use them.)

You can make a difference. On December 28, 1989, two days before Portland began its ban on polystyrene foam in restaurants, McDonald's filed a lawsuit against this ordinance. McDonald's lost. Less than ten months later this same international fast-food company banned the use of polystyrene foam from all its restaurants. You can bet the boardrooms of Kentucky Fried Chicken and Burger King were buzzing over McDonald's positive environmental image.

Oregon is considered an environmental leader. Right now we have one of the nation's best recycling records, 20 percent, but the amount of garbage produced in Portland over the last six years has increased by 54 percent. The Public Land Act protects Oregon beaches, but in 1992 our ocean will be available for offshore drilling. The native forests of the Northwest are the world's largest storehouses of carbon per acre, yet two square miles of the oldest and largest trees are clearcut each week.

> *...found the woods so thick with under groth that the hunters could not get any distance into the Isld. the red wood, and Green bryers interwoven, and mixed with pine, alder, a Specis of Beech, ash &c. we killed nothing today.*
>
> GEORGE ROGERS CLARK
> ON THE COLUMBIA RIVER, NOVEMBER 6, 1805

This directory is a start for those who want to make environmental changes. We would like to see this book updated annually, and we invite you to fill out the form at the end to advise us of new products, services, and organizations that will help us all save Oregon.

*h*OW TO USE THIS DIRECTORY ....

> *Man corrupt everything, say Shug. He on your box of grits, in your head, and all over the radio. He try to make you think he everywhere. Soon as you think he everywhere, you think he God. But he ain't. Whenever you trying to pray and man plop himself on the other end of it, tell him to git lost, say Shug. Conjure up flowers, wind, water, a big rock.*
>
> ALICE WALKER, *THE COLOR PURPLE*

Save Oregon is divided into two sections. Part One, the information section, briefly discusses environmental issues that affect us as Oregonians and citizens of the world. For example the average dosage of herbicide applied to our lawns is five times greater than the amount sprayed on agricultural crops. As we identify each problem we offer suggestions, such as how to build a better grass root system through correct watering, aeration, and fertilization; even organic ways to destroy those pesky dandelions.

Part Two is an alphabetical index of local products and services—which garden shops have organic lawn fertilizers, who stocks unbleached paper, how to connect with environmental groups. Many sections end with mail-order sources from around the country. Where practical we have given prices for the sake of comparison, although these are subject to change.

When citing numerous Oregon outlets we divided the state into geographic sections—standardly Willamette Valley, Southern Oregon, Eastern and Central Oregon, and the Coast. For most items we found outlets under all four. Under these headings we have listed cities alphabetically. Area code 503 applies to all the Oregon phone numbers.

You can turn to the table of contents or index for the category that interests you most, or read the text in Part One that will refer you to the appropriate listings in Part Two. Either way, we think this directory will prove as invaluable to you as it is to us.

part one
STEPS TO SAVING OREGON

*e*NERGY CONSERVATION.................................

> *The sea changed, the fields changed, the rivers, the villages, and the people changed.*
> THOMAS HARDY, *TESS OF THE D'URBERVILLES*

The greenhouse effect is caused by a blanket of gas that traps the sun's heat. The PBS series "Race to Save the Planet" compared this phenomenon to a car parked in the sun. Light passes through the front windshield, and when it strikes objects it becomes heat. Light in the form of heat has difficulty escaping back through the glass, and therefore the temperature inside the car rises.

A layer of greenhouse gas has always existed. It keeps our planet warm, and without it the earth would be cold and barren. But in the past there was a wonderful balance, as if the side windows on our imaginary car were rolled down and some heat could escape. Because carbon dioxide, chlorofluorocarbons (CFCs), nitrous oxide, and methane trap heat, those side windows are slowly rolling up.

Climatologists, with predictive computer models of the consequences of global warming, make clear that part of the controversy comes from the play of unknown factors. We can predict that warmer bodies of water will result in more clouds. If the clouds are low, they will cool the earth and help counter the greenhouse effect; if the clouds are high, they will trap more heat. It becomes a game of Russian roulette.

Four of the warmest years in this century occurred during the 1980s. The years 1980 and 1988 were the hottest ever, then 1990 was, and we have survived. But what happens in fifty or sixty years if these projections are right, and average temperatures rise three to ten degrees?

According to computer models, with such a rise almost every country would lose valuable coastal land. In the United States the ocean would flood Cape Cod, Louisiana, Florida, and Long Island. If the ocean rises only one foot, ten miles of land can be lost along its circumference. The Midwest would suffer long dry summers. Crops would wither. Entire world food supplies would shift. Forests, marooned in the wrong climate, would die, and as wildlife lost its ecosystems the animals would be trapped by highways and cities, and could not migrate.

> *I was born upon the prarie, where the wind blew free, and there was nothing to break the light of the sun. I was born where there were no enclosures, and where everything drew a free breath. I want to die there, and not within walls.*
> TEN BEARS, COMANCHE, 1872

The World Watch Institute warns that the most threatening environmental problems are the result of burning fossil fuels. Carbon dioxide is responsible for 50 percent of the greenhouse effect, and the United States is responsible for 22 percent of the world's carbon dioxide emissions. David Brook, Oregon Extension Service energy agent, devised the table on the following page so you can calculate how many trees need to be planted to offset the amount of carbon dioxide you use each year.

The massive burning of rain forests creates carbon dioxide, as it reduces the number of trees available to reuse carbon dioxide. Twenty percent of global warming can be blamed on methane. Besides that produced by livestock in farming, methane is produced in the flooded soils of rice paddies and in landfills when organic wastes break down—another reason to recycle. Nitrous oxide results when chemical fertilizers break down in the soil, so it's important to garden organically and to support organic farmers by buying their products (see Food, Organic Produce).

The less fuel we burn, the less we contribute to global warming. Saving fossil fuel is the most important conservation step we can take, and in many ways the easiest. It doesn't require us to dramatically change life style—no need to huddle in dark, cold caves. Purchase wisely, save energy, save money. We based the table of savings below from simple actions on information from "Race to Save the Planet."

Simple Actions That Save Fossil Fuel

ACTION	SAVED PER YEAR	
	ENERGY	DOLLARS
Lowering water heater temperature to 115-120°	15%	$25
Fastening jacket on water heater	17%	$55
Installing low-flow shower head	70%	$115

CO_2 EMISSIONS FROM ALL YOUR PERSONAL ENERGY USES

CO_2 Emission from Cars and Trucks

	YOUR PRESENT VEHICLE	POSSIBLE NEW VEHICLE
1. Total miles driven each year:	_____ mi.	_____ mi.
2. Efficiency of vehicle (average miles per gallon):	÷ _____ mpg	÷ _____ mpg
3. Estimated gallons of gas consumed:	= _____ gal.	= _____ gal.
4. CO_2 released per gallon of gas used:	× 20 lb. CO_2/gal.*	× 20 lb. CO_2/gal.
5. Annual CO_2 you produce from driving:	= _____ lb. CO_2/year	= _____ lb. CO_2/year

*CO_2 conversions are from the Oregon Department of Energy.

CO_2 Emissions from Home Energy Use

	ELECTRIC	GAS, OIL, PROPANE AND WOOD
1. Last year's total energy costs: Don't include monthly base charges, usually $3–5/month	$	$
2. Cost per fuel unit: Oregon average costs: $0.045/kWh for home electric use $0.058/therm for home natural gas use Check a recent utility bill or call your utility to find out your cost. For oil, LP gas/propane, and wood, enter cost per fuel unit from bills.	÷ $ _____ per kWh	÷ $ _____ per therm, gal., lb., cord
3. Total home energy used in fuel units: Divide line 1 by line 2 for electricity and natural gas. For oil, LP gas/propane, and wood, enter total fuel units from bills	= _____ kWh	= _____ therm, gal., lb., cord
4. Amount of CO_2 produced per unit of fuel used: Enter amounts from this list. Natural gas = 12 lb. CO_2 per therm #2 heating oil = 22.5 lb. CO_2 per gal. LP gas/propane = 13.8 lb. CO_2 per gal. Wood = 1600 lb. CO_2 per cord (average) Electricity = 2.5 lb. CO_2 per kWh if 100% of the electricity is produced from coal-fired plants. (Oregon statewide average is 10% = 0.25 lb. per kWh. Ask your electric utility what percent of the electricity it distributes is generated from coal.)	× _____ lb. CO_2/kWh	× _____ lb. CO_2/therm, gal., lb., cord
5. Annual CO_2 you produce from home energy use: Multiply total fuel units in line 3 by their line 4 factors.	= _____ lb. CO_2/year from electricity	= _____ lb. CO_2/year from combustion

Totals

1. Grand total amount of CO_2 produced by
   your household per year: ____ lb. CO_2 per year
   Combine all CO_2 totals from first two sections.
2. Average amount of CO_2 fixed by a tree
   each year: ÷ 26 lb. CO_2 per tree per year
   Green plants fix carbon from CO_2, taking it out
   of the atmosphere.
3. Number of trees you'd need to plant to
   offset this amount of CO_2:   = ____ trees

Now are you convinced?

Concern for man himself and for his fate must always form the chief interest of all technical endeavors...in order that the creations of our minds shall be a blessing not a curse for mankind.
                                          ALBERT EINSTEIN

Over its lifetime one compact fluorescent lamp will avoid the release of a ton of carbon dioxide and twenty pounds of sulfur oxide (a cause of acid rain). A seventy-five-watt light bulb lasts a thousand hours. An eighteen-watt compact fluorescent bulb (CFB) lasts ten thousand hours and will save up to $40 on your electric bill. Don't let the $12 to $18 price per bulb stop you, and don't let the word fluorescent prejudice you—CFBs don't have the humming blue flicker of fluorescent tubes. The only drawback is that they shouldn't be used with dimmers or in enclosed fixtures.

There are two kinds of CFBs. SLs have adapters attached to the bulb, and PLs need a separate adapter. Pacific Lamp recommends using SLs for the home and PLs for businesses or in situations when your light will be left on for extended periods.

The following facts from the Izaak Walton League show that when you buy a compact fluorescent light bulb you save:

- the purchase and disposal of nine standard light bulbs;

- thirty-three dollars in electricity costs (based on Portland rates);

- plus one of these:

- consumption of 1.3 barrels of oil in an oil-burning power plant (enough to drive an economy car across the United States);
- consumption of 528 pounds of coal in a coal-burning power plant, with the production of 1,600 pounds of carbon dioxide greenhouse gases and 21 pounds of sulfur dioxide, which cause acid rain;
- the creation of about one curie of high-level nuclear waste and use of 25 milligrams of plutonium in a nuclear power plant.

Ways to conserve energy include to:

- Insulate your home with weatherstripping.
- Use insulated glass, window film, white reflective window shades, or heavy drapes, especially on large windows or glass doors.
- Lower the thermostat to sixty-eight degrees in winter, and to fifty-five degrees or less when you're sleeping or away from home for more than four hours.
- Wash clothes with warm or cold water, and rinse in cold.
- Eliminate the drying cycle on your dishwasher.
- Run the dishwasher only when it's full.
- Turn off the television and other appliances when you're not using them.
- Replace incandescent light bulbs with compact fluorescent bulbs wherever possible.

One reason we use so much fuel is that heat leaks out through glass windows and doors, even through electrical outlets. By replacing plain glass in sliding doors and windows with insulated glass, or using insulated drapes to cover them, you can keep heat out during the summer and in during the winter. While hunting for good window and door insulation, we also found window film and window tinting that reduce glare, block almost all ultraviolet rays, and reflect solar heat. All these are listed in Part Two under Insulation.

Weatherstripping can be found in most hardware and home supply stores. We've found one that's nontoxic and will last for the life of your home. It resists fungus and mildew and is not affected by sunlight, ultraviolet light, or chemicals. Weatherstripping is also listed under Insulation.

Before you invest in expensive weatherization such as thermal pane windows or insulation, have an audit of your current energy use. Let an expert decide which steps will save you the most money and energy. See Free Energy Audits under Weatherization.

Our addiction to fossil fuels remains unabated even after repeated oil crises. A big step in energy conservation and efficiency can be taken with nonpolluting alternative energy sources, but government and industry need to be pushed toward their development. Since 1980 federal funding of research and development for solar energy has dropped 90 percent, while solar energy generation has become 73 percent more efficient. Creation of global warming gases and acid rain would decrease dramatically if we shifted our means of energy production.

Luckily, some states provide incentives for this shift. Oregon offers an Alternative Energy Device (AED) tax rebate for solar, wind, hydroelectric, and geothermal power sources. Heat your house, warm your bath water, and play your stereo without producing carbon dioxide. Become your own utility.

Solar energy is used for heating and electrical generation. Solar collectors on your roof can cut your hot-water bill by 65 percent. Attach a south-facing solarium or greenhouse to your house and you will see a reduction in your heating bill. Photovoltaic panels make electricity directly from light even in cloudy weather and, once installed, last indefinitely with little maintenance. Other energy sources are site specific, but sunlight is around every day.

For information on solar tax rebates, water and space heating, and photovoltaics check under Solar Energy. For details on wind see Wind Power. On individuals' use of hydroelectric and geothermal sources there is still too little to report.

Soon your mighty forest trees, under the shade of whose wide spreading branches you

> *have played in infancy, sported in boyhood, and now rest your wearied limbs after the fatigue of the chase, will be cut down to fence in the land which the white intruders dare to call their own.*
>
> — TECUMSEH, SHAWNEE, 1811

We've all appreciated the girth of a redwood or the spread of a noble fir. But trees are also life sustainers—the protectors of our soil and the most practical defense against the greenhouse effect.

Trees use carbon dioxide (CO_2) like we use oxygen, in the process converting it to the oxygen we need. Three mature trees can transform fifty pounds of carbon dioxide into oxygen each year. But protecting our existing trees is not enough—to sustain the lifetime oxygen requirements of one child, more than three hundred trees must be planted.

We hear about the massacre of forests in other countries, but according to the Native Forest Council less than 5 percent of our nation's original native forests remains today. Brazil retains 85 percent of its forests, and Japan, by importing lumber from Oregon, preserves 26 percent. Less than 1 percent of our nation's remaining forests are protected from logging.

Television is peppered with advertisements showing tree seedlings packed into the ground, while the announcer assures us these will sprout into tomorrow's wilderness. But these seedlings are single-species plants, and the resulting tree plantations will have as much biodiversity as a cornfield.

> *In wildness is the preservation of the world.*
>
> — HENRY DAVID THOREAU

A single inch of topsoil takes five hundred years to form, and the world loses twenty-five billion tons of topsoil each year. Trees are our best protection against the erosive power of rain and wind. A forest stops wind from swirling up soil, and rain from washing those precious inches of ground into our rivers.

*r*ecycling ....

> *Garbage is the only raw material that we're too stupid to use.*
>
> ARTHUR C. CLARK

Every state in the Union deposits some of its waste stream in other states. Part of Oregon's hazardous waste travels to Alabama. But we receive much more waste than we ship out; in fact, garbage from Washington state will soon reach one million tons per year, and compounding that disadvantage, controversy is brewing whether Washington should continue to pay low Oregon rates.

Last year Portland generated 962,000 tons of garbage, and in the last six years landfill fees have zoomed from eight dollars per ton to forty-five dollars per ton. Portland's landfills are so chock-full, garbage must be trucked 140 miles up the Columbia Gorge.

The solution to brimming landfills is obvious. Recycle. Not only will it solve the garbage crisis, but almost every environmental problem—the greenhouse effect, deforestation, air and water pollution—is reduced through recycling.

It takes 95 percent less energy to manufacture aluminum from recycled cans than from ore. Recycling glass bottles uses less water and energy, decreases air pollution, and reduces mining wastes by 80 percent. Each ton of recycled paper saves seventeen trees, seven thousand gallons of water, and 4,100 kilowatt-hours of electricity.

Take the first step. Designate an area where you can collect recyclables. Set up bags or boxes in your kitchen, porch, utility room, or basement. It's much easier if you sort as you go.

Take the second step. Find out what you can recycle where. Thanks to an Oregon law any city with a population of more than four thousand must provide monthly curb recycling for some items. The Metro Recycling Information Center suggests the following ways to prepare for your curbside pickup:

1. Bundle up **newspapers** with a string or pack them in a brown paper bag.

2. Rinse **glass** and sort it by color. Labels don't have to be removed, and metal lids can be placed with tin cans.

3. Rinse **tin cans** and remove both ends and the label. If possible flatten them.

4. Flatten and tie **cardboard boxes** together with a string. **Brown paper bags** should be placed in this pile.

5. No-deposit **aluminum** cans, foil, pie plates, TV dinner trays, old window frames, and patio furniture should be clean and broken into manageable pieces. Return all your beverage aluminum cans for deposit.

6. Place **used motor oil** in a nonbreakable, tightly sealed container (such as a plastic milk jug). Do not mix it with anything else.

7. Save **scrap metal** (such as nails, bolts, and screws) in a sturdy container.

Who will take plastic and which plastics they'll accept changes almost daily. With the phone numbers listed under Recycling Contact People, you can obtain this information for every area in the state. Once you know which plastics are accepted, check the bottom of potential purchases (arrows surround a number that indicates type) and select plastic containers for recyclability.

The same recycling contact people have information about Styrofoam, tires, appliances, office paper, magazines, and hazardous wastes. If you're unsure whether something is a hazardous waste read the label for such clue words as flammable, caustic, corrosive, caution, danger, warning, or poison.

> *We make our lives rich by making our wants few.*
>
> **HENRY DAVID THOREAU**

Take the third step. Buy in bulk and look for products with little packaging. If you don't have your own compost pile, haul those yard clippings to someone who will turn them into compost, and buy recycled compost to support these recyclers. Any time you buy recycled products you're encouraging more recycling depots to appear in your area.

How much of your mail do you read, and how much do you throw away? Write to the Mail Preference Service at the Direct Marketing Association, 6 E. 43rd Street, New York, NY 10017-4646, and request that you be taken off junk mail lists. When you receive a catalog that you won't use, make a copy of the following note and send it off.

> **Dear People:**
>
> **I appreciate you sending me your catalogs, but you may have noticed I don't place orders with your company. I am more interested in reducing waste paper and saving trees than receiving future catalogs. Please take me off your list, and do not give my name to any other company. Thank you.**

Every household could save a tree and a half a year by eliminating junk mail.

WATER POLLUTION

> *Brush your teeth with the best toothpaste. Then rinse your mouth with industrial waste.*
>
> TOM LEHRER

Deadly "Agent Orange," the defoliant used in Vietnam, is one of the most familiar dioxins. When paper is bleached with chlorine, dioxins are formed. These carcinogenic chemicals are in the wastes that pulp mills leak into rivers, in our coffee filters and milk cartons, and therefore in the liquids we drink. Most North American nursing mothers now have dioxin in their milk.

The early test results from an EPA calculation have revealed that pulp mills may be spewing eight times more dioxin into the Columbia River than the current water quality standard recommends. At Twilight Eagle Sanctuary, in Astoria on the Columbia River, the eagles weren't reproducing at their expected rate. Toxins were found in the eagles and in their eggshells.

> *The buffalo are diminishing fast. The antelope, that were plenty a few years ago, they are now thin. When they shall all die we shall be hungry....*
>
> TALL BULL, CHEYENNE, 1867

Unless we buy unbleached, recycled paper products, dioxin pollution will increase, but industry can't be blamed for all our murky waters. Sixty-five percent of water pollution comes from automobile oils and agricultural chemicals. Imagine the rain on a lawn mixing with pesticides and herbicides, or melted snow in a parking lot blending with oil and gasoline. What underground water has passed through, it has picked up. According to the organization Earth Day, the amount of motor oil alone that finds its way into streams, rivers, and oceans each year is equal to sixteen Exxon *Valdez* oil spills.

In December of 1988 Milwaukie, Oregon found trichloroethylene (TCE) in all seven of its wells. The wells were shut down. Three years later five wells are still closed. Milwaukie buys part of its water from Portland and has completed two packed aeration towers to treat its TCE-contaminated wells. Years ago TCE was used in septic tanks, and although the specific source of Milwaukie's TCE has not been discovered, the state Department of Environmental Quality is investigating this possible source.

Some people have turned to bottled water, but the standards for bottled water are similar to EPA standards for tap water, and the energy costs for packaging and shipping outweigh some of the advantages. Water-purifying systems block some chemicals but usually don't stop the really dangerous pollutants. Before you take the costly precaution of buying one, find out if it's necessary by having your water tested (look in the Yellow Pages under Environmental Services).

> *Roll on, thou deep and dark blue Ocean—Roll!*
> *Ten thousand fleets sweep over thee in vain;*
> *Man marks the earth with ruin—his control*

Stops with the shore.
LORD BYRON, "SONNET ON CHILLON"

Somehow we feel the vastness of the Pacific Ocean should dilute any pollution. The Environmental Defense Fund discovered that 90 percent of the shrimp caught off the U.S. coast are contaminated with marine paint residues. On any Oregon beach you can see the backwash of Styrofoam and plastic six-pack "nooses." There have been wonderful efforts to clean debris from Oregon beaches, but how do we clean the debris in our oceans? And what will happen in 1992 if we permit offshore drilling?

What can we do?

Become active in environmental groups that lobby against offshore drilling. Buy unbleached, recycled paper products. Replace petroleum-based garden chemicals with organic products that don't leach into the groundwater. Support local legislation that restricts industrial wastes; see the listings under Political Information and Environmental Action Groups. Report water polluters; we supply local numbers for you to call under Pollution Complaints.

We must stop using toxic chemicals and properly dispose of the hazardous waste we do use; call the information sources for hazardous waste under Recycling. Used oil can be cleaned and made into a lubricant. One gallon of used motor oil will produce two and a half quarts of lubrication oil, which you can buy; see Recycled Products on the Market. If all recycled motor oil were made into lubricant we could save 1.3 million barrels of oil every day.

Phosphates promote algae growth, and green slime now scums the Tualatin River and the Columbia Slough. The fish there are starving for oxygen. The Metropolitan Service District responded to this problem and banned detergents with phosphates in the Portland area.

A statewide ban on phosphates will be introduced in the Oregon legislature in 1991. Fred Meyer, Inc. supports this ban and has already restocked all its detergent shelves with phosphate-free products.

Biodegradable soaps, detergents, and cleansers can replace products that have chemical pollutants. Many of the preferable products are available in local stores. If none of the grass-roots stores under Cleaning Supplies is near you, use our mail-order listings, or buy one of the milder soaps and cleansers: Ivory Snow, Fels Naptha, Arm & Hammer, and good old Bon Ami.

Remember that what goes down your drain does not magically disappear; eventually it will come back through your faucet.

*W*ATER CONSERVATION ....

> *Oregonians don't tan*
> *They just rust.*
>
> T-SHIRT

During the 1970s Governor Tom McCall discouraged population growth by exaggerating Oregon's rainfall. T-shirts described webfooted Oregonians and warned that looking at Oregon skies could result in drowning. In the Willamette Valley our hallways puddle up from wet umbrellas, and when the gray drizzle finally lifts, we're stunned by the lush green of our landscape. How could Oregon have a water shortage?

> *Rained all the after part of last night, rain continues this morning, I slept but verry little last night for the noise Kept up dureing the whole of the night by the Swans, Geese, white & Grey Brant Ducks....*
>
> GEORGE ROGERS CLARK
ON THE COLUMBIA RIVER, NOVEMBER 1805

Much of Oregon is desert and scrub grass. Even in the Willamette Valley, because of population growth there are projected water shortages for the early part of the next century, especially in Washington County. A dam has been proposed on the Tualatin River. This costly project is not expected to include the several million dollars required for a fish ladder, and if a dam is built without one the winter steelhead and coho salmon could no longer migrate.

Water conservation protects wetlands and the habitats of fish and animals. When water flow is low the chance of water contamination increases. Because of global warming and water pollution the likelihood of drought increases each year. It's worth trudging through that winter downpour to buy a low-flow shower head.

You may eventually put a number of water-saving plans into effect, but the step you take today brings us all closer to our goal. Don't be overwhelmed by the enormity of the problem. Concentrate on the step you're taking, and repeat that step every day. Then add another.

It's not enough to stop washing your car at home with a hose (which uses up to one hundred fifty gallons of water) or to switch to self-service car washes (five to ten gallons) or a bucket and sponge (about fifteen gallons). It's not enough to shut off your water faucet while brushing your teeth, saving approximately nine gallons every brushing. These things will help, of course, but we must do more. For instance, we've found an effective way to wash cars using only one gallon of water. It's listed under Water Conservation Products.

Our eating habits influence the water shortage. More water is used to irrigate pasture that feeds cattle and sheep than to grow other agricultural crops. It takes fifty-five square feet of pasture to produce one hamburger. Also, animal wastes are not treated in sewage systems and do seep into our groundwater—another reason to eat lower on the food chain.

Face it. Many of the appliances we use gulp down hundreds of gallons of water each week, though water-conserving dishwashers and washing machines are becoming more prevalent. Most water waste occurs in the bathroom. When you start to make changes, remember that everything you save counts.

> *...where the sun beats...*
> *And the dry stone no sounds of water*
> *...I will show you fear in a handful of dust.*
> — T. S. ELIOT, "THE WASTELAND"

Use a plastic toilet dam. It prevents one to four gallons of water from leaving your tank each time you flush. Most hardware stores carry them, and they're available by mail order through catalogs listed under Publications. Instead of using a dam you can set a plastic jug of water inside your tank. Please don't use bricks—they often disintegrate and cause more problems than they solve.

A device we've found called the Royal Flush, a Water Restrictor under Water Conservation Products, is not a dam and is easily installed in any toilet tank. It has a two-way handle that allows you to push down for one-quarter flush or up for a full flush. The one-quarter flush uses one gallon of water and works so effectively you may not need to use the full-flush option.

If you live in one of the drier Oregon regions or you're dependent on well water, you might install an ultra-low-flow toilet. Most plumbing supply stores can order them. One of the most popular and reliable brands is Toto, made and used successfully in Japan for years.

The average person uses more than twenty gallons of water showering each day. If your home is less than three years old you're already showering with a low-flow shower head. Oregon requires them in all new homes, and they're the only shower head available on the Oregon market. If your shower head is older than three years, replace it or put a water flow restrictor between the shower head and the pipe (for fifty cents to a dollar, at hardware stores). Vacuum breakers can be attached to American-made hand-held units and add-on restrictors to European hand-held units. If you miss that morning gush of shower water try a Spa 2000, listed under Shower Heads, Low Flow. It puts so much air in the water you'll feel deliciously wasteful.

For a dollar or two also buy water restrictors for your indoor water faucets. They aerate the water for a soft flow (no splash) and restrict maximum usage to three gallons a minute. They're especially effective if someone in your family confuses "on" with "full blast." Most hardware stores carry them. Ask your hardware store about water restrictors for dishwashers; they're starting to appear on the market.

Before you take a long trip, turn off your water and hot water heater. The Portland environmental store If Not Now...When? sells a gadget that turns off your hot water heater automatically every night.

Garbage disposals use a lot of water, besides adding solids to overloaded sewer systems. Instead, compost your garbage. Don't leave the rinse water running when you hand-wash your dishes, and make sure your automatic dishwasher is crammed full before you switch it on.

Check for leaks. If your water meter dial moves when no water is being used, you have a leak. Add colored water to the tank of your toilet, and don't flush for thirty minutes. If colored water seeps into the bowl, it's leaking.

Gray water is the leftover water from showers, tubs, and kitchen sinks. Use biodegradable, phosphate-free soaps and detergents (and a plug) and this water can be scooped out and reused on plants—that is, if your plants don't object. Some do. Soaps and detergents turn water alkaline, and acid-loving citrus plus many shade plants, azaleas, and ferns should not be watered with gray water. Neither should vegetables, nor edible plants.

A Water Cycle Rinse Recycle System allows you to divert your washing machine rinse water into a holding tank, where it's pumped into your drip irrigation system or underground perforated pipe. As gray water, this should be used immediately on ornamental plants, not food crops. The Recycler is listed under Water Conservation Products.

We did find one product, Bi-O-Kleen, that is used as both a produce wash and detergent. Not only is its gray water safe for edible plants, but people who have used it over long periods claim it acts like a fertilizer. For more information on gray water and plants consult the handbook listed under Water Conservation Products.

Whether you have a xeriscape (drought-tolerant garden), a vegetable garden, or a lush garden of water-thirsty plants, you can conserve water by using drip irrigation systems, water timers, and soaker hoses.

Drip irrigation is flexible black polyethylene tubing or PVC pipe fitted with emitters, soakers, or sprayers that dispense water slowly. You can customize the emitters to fit your garden's needs. Soaker hoses are flexible rubber hoses that allow water to weep through tiny openings. Both drip and soaker watering systems can be laid above or buried below ground and can be found in hardware stores or through mail-order catalogs. You can find them both listed under Water Conservation Products. Automated water timers are also listed in this section; they turn your drip system or sprinkler automatically on and off, work at one or more locations, and allow you to program a number of different watering times a week.

The best garden hose nozzles shut off automatically when you're not squeezing the trigger, and there are models that have water restrictors built in them. Limit your watering time to morning or late afternoon, when the least water is lost through evaporation (morning is best to avoid mildew).

To retain moisture add peat moss to your soil. Most commercial soil moisture retainers are made from plastic polymers, and their residues may affect microorganisms in the soil. Down to Earth (a distributor and retailer) offers Sta-Wet, a moisture retainer made with starch polymers. It can be used in the soil or on indoor and outdoor potted plants. Sta-Wet remains in the soil from one to two years.

The American quest for the perfect lawn squanders water and poisons the soil with herbicides. Organic Lawn Care, a lawn maintenance company, suggests you minimize this environmental damage with aerated soil, which can retain up to 75 percent more water. Encourage aeration with organic fertilizers, which restore the soil's natural microscopic life (chemical fertilizers kill these natural disease-destroying elements). Then water only when your grass starts to wilt; this encourages deep root penetration and helps stress tolerance. Since city water contains chlorine, which also kills beneficial microorganisms, overwatering can harm your lawn.

> *I was determined to know beans.*
> **HENRY DAVID THOREAU**

Think up creative alternatives to lawns. Our personal quest is to replace stretches of boring green with paths, flowers, and just a patch of lawn to sprawl on. Last year in the middle of our vegetable garden we planted a succulent bed, our desert in an oasis. The side of our house is a mass of wildflowers, and two beds grow nothing but herbs. Our thirsty perennial beds are covered with Ringer's organically safe landscape cloth, which cuts down watering and smothers weeds. This year we plan to replace more sod with Native Oregon Plants—many outlets are listed here under that heading—which require half the watering. We'd rather pick bouquets of flowers than mow the lawn.

CLEAN AIR AND TRANSPORTATION

> *Fair is foul, and foul is fair:*
> *Hover through the fog and filthy air.*
> **SHAKESPEARE, THE WITCHES IN *MACBETH***

When Los Angeles youths were autopsied, 80 percent had lung abnormalities and 20 percent severe lung lesions. Smog.

Yes, Oregon is not LA, but on smoggy days our eyes burn, we feel tired, and breathing becomes difficult. Most smog comes from ground-level ozone (gas formed when sunlight combines with hydrocarbons and nitrous oxide). Utility, chemical, and oil plants release these chemicals.

Thanks to the Community Right to Know Law, in 1988 the state fire marshall's office and the federal Environmental Protection Agency (EPA) released a set of statistics about chemical pollution in Oregon. These figures don't tell the whole story since they include only the state's largest chemical emitters and 325 chemicals out of a possible 40,000. Chemicals that have been released into the air through evaporation and chimneys now total 21,918,126 pounds. Our waterways contain 597,076 pounds. Chemicals amounting to 8,145,135 pounds have been absorbed by land and public sewage, which will eventually reach our underground water systems. And the amount of chemicals collected for hazardous wastes sites amounts to 11,852,402 pounds.

Automobiles are one of the biggest culprits in air pollution. We can cut emissions by ride sharing and using buses or driving gas-efficient cars; see Public Transportation and Automobiles and Scooters, Energy Efficient. Or ride a bicycle, or walk. Plan your day's travels so you needn't double-back. Carpool.

There are products that reduce car pollution. The MHD Fuel Conditioner Unit claims to cut hydrocarbon and carbon monoxide pollution. An activated carbon filter removes hydrocarbons and other contaminants from the air that flows through your automobile. It's listed under Automobile Products, Smog Reduction.

Proper automobile maintenance is a must. A well-tuned engine cuts emissions, and well-inflated radial tires increase fuel efficiency even further. Fix your muffler if it's damaged. And look for alternate routes that are less congested, or try to drive at less congested times of day. Idling engines spew three hundred times as much carbon monoxide into the air as those running at full speed. Remind your gas station attendant not to "top off" your gas tank, so benzene does not leak into the air. And report smoking vehicles or industrial pollution, as described under Pollution Complaints.

> *Love is a lie, until you prove it to be true.*
> *Marriage is a lie until you prove it to be true.*
> *Earth care is a lie, too, until you prove it true.*
>
> RAY BRADBURY

There are so many little things we can do. When we consider global warming, ozone depletion, and vanishing species, our actions seem like nickel-dime efforts. But if all these nickel-dime efforts are multiplied by millions of concerned people they approach solutions.

An average home gives off more than four tons of carbon dioxide per year and other pollutants from the by-products of electrical generation. When you turn off electrical appliances, insulate your home, or use solar energy, you decrease air pollution.

If you have furniture made of particle board, own clothes made of permanent-press fabrics, or save paper grocery bags, there's probably formaldehyde in your home. Benzene is found in plastic, rubber, and some detergents. Dry-cleaned clothes usually have residues from trichloroethylene (a chemical implicated in liver cancer). House plants help purify the air and, according to NASA, may turn formaldehyde, benzene, and trichloroethylene into oxygen. NASA found that the gerbera daisy and philodendron are two of the best air cleaners.

Even if you breath the pristine air of the Wallowa Mountains, what contaminates the world contaminates you, and eventually contaminates your children. The poisons we let escape into our air have been shredding great holes in the ozone layer, a shield high above the earth that protects us from solar ultraviolet radiation.

In 1985 scientists discovered an ozone hole the size of the United States above Antarctica. Several years later this depleted ozone drifted across Australia. During the Australian spring of 1988 ozone values dropped 12 percent for one month. Crops and fish populations were affected, and some doctors predict two out of three Australians will have some form of skin cancer before age seventy. The percentage of ozone over the Arctic is decreasing now, and this lack will harm both Europe and North America.

Chlorofluorocarbons (CFCs) are the major cause of ozone depletion, and of 20 percent of the greenhouse effect. They have been used for fast-food containers (Styrofoam), aerosols, foam insulation, and refrigerator and air conditioner coolant.

Portland has banned the use of CFC containers by restaurants and food services. McDonald's recently announced that their Big Macs will no longer come in CFC packages. Others need to be pressed to follow these examples.

What we put in our air does not keep hovering over us. Eastern Canadian forests are dying from acid rain largely produced by U.S. industry in the Midwest, and our country is responsible for almost a fourth of the world's carbon dioxide emissions. At a recent United Nations conference on global warming eighteen of the largest industrial nations agreed to stabilize or reduce greenhouse gases by the year 2000. The United States refused to sign the treaty. Even in the Mediterranean, environmental treaties have been signed between such fierce enemies as the Greeks and Turks and the Israelis and Arabs. A child born in the United States uses thirty times more natural resources than a child born in India. Our pollution pollutes the world, and it is time to take responsibility.

Check your air conditioner. If it's leaking, CFCs are entering the atmosphere. One charge of Freon from your air conditioner will contribute as much to global warming as the amount of carbon dioxide emitted from a new car driven twenty thousand miles.

In Oregon those who service your car air conditioner must recycle the coolant. The Oregon State Public Interest Research Group (OSPIRG) drafted the bill establishing this, and only two other states, Vermont and Hawaii, have similar laws. OSPIRG wants to expand legislation on coolants. CFC-free insulation, like fiberglass and cellulose (see Recycled Products), is available. If you buy a fire extinguisher, make sure it doesn't contain Halon.

What will happen in Oregon if we don't curb air pollution? There is no need to spin out science fiction possibilities; the future of any air-polluted city is apparent in the bans proposed by the South Coast Air Quality District for Los Angeles and Orange counties and parts of Riverside, San Bernadino, and Ventura counties. They include stiff fines and rules governing automobiles—by the summer of 1991 every business with more than one hundred employees must institute carpooling or be subject to a $25,000 fine. During the second phase of the plan 40 percent of the passenger vehicles, 70 percent of the trucks, and all buses will be required to use "low-emitting" fuels, such as methanol, and by 2007 a ban is sought on all gasoline engines.

Political analysts have never been able to peg Oregon as liberal or conservative—they usually throw their hands in the air and say "independent." Oregonians appreciate the beauty of their state, but they don't like rules. The best way to support both these ideals is to take care of pollution now.

There's so much to do, but making changes does not have to feel like sacrifice. It can give us the right perspective, the feeling that our destinies are linked to the earth.

> *Cowardice asks the question, Is it safe?*
> *Expediency asks the question, Is it politic?*
> *Vanity asks the question, Is it popular?*
> *But conscience asks the question, Is it right?*
> *And there comes a time when one must take a position that is neither safe, nor politic, nor popular, but he must take it because his conscience tells him that it is right....*
> —MARTIN LUTHER KING, JR.

*e*NVIRONMENTALLY SMART PRODUCTS ....

> *Modern man seems to believe he can get everything he needs from the supermarket and corner drugstore. He doesn't understand that everything has a source in the land or sea, and that he must respect these sources.*
> THOR HEYERDAHL

On old television commercials gorillas pummeled luggage, and watches strapped to boat propellers whirled through water. Products were touted as durable. Now it's a virtue if you use it once and toss it out. We buy quantity—whole packages of razors—instead of quality. Even cameras are disposable. Landfills brim and smokestacks spew so we can buy more and more that lasts less and less long.

This section describes products that conserve natural resources and are nontoxic to our bodies and our earth. The list is not complete, but rather a beginning. Every day new products appear on the market, and they'll show up faster when manufacturers know we're serious about purchasing them. When safe products appear in your supermarkets, tell the store managers you appreciate their effort. If you can't find certain products, ask that they be stocked. We have enormous power to change the environment, and that power is in our wallets.

Also ask managers to put up special displays highlighting earth-friendly merchandise. Safeway, based on manufacturer claims and some testing, marks the environmental attributes of its merchandise. This doesn't mean everything about the product is sound, only that the package is recycled or the detergent doesn't have phosphates. Some Safeway stores are experimenting too with meat packages that don't use Styrofoam.

The "Green Cross" label at Fred Meyer stores means a product has been tested by a not-for-profit environmental company. Not only must the product be environmentally safe but the package and the manufacturing process must have met high standards. Right now about fifty products have passed these stringent tests; you can feel comfortable buying them. Payless has just come out with its own earth-friendly label.

Recycling wastes is important, but in a sense, it comes too late. You've already bought and consumed natural resources and energy when you consume something manufactured with virgin raw materials. An even more important step in environmental consciousness is to avoid consuming such products at all. When you buy reusable razors, refillable pens, and cloth coffee filters you've short-circuited the waste cycle.

Consider the package. Is it smothered in plastic layers? Is it made from recycled material? If you buy the economy size, you've bought one package, not two. Many stores now offer grains, cereals, and other products in bulk.

Some of the small grass-roots stores have amazing bulk sections. The Oasis in Eugene offers more than four hundred different bulk items. Such stores even have giant containers of syrups, oils, soaps, and cosmetic products. Instead of buying that plastic container of hair conditioner each month, you bring back your bottle and refill it. They're wonderful products, most have not been animal tested, and they offer another chance to support the small merchant who struggled for years to sell environmental merchandise before it became popular.

The need to replace old familiar products with environmentally safe alternatives may seem overwhelming at first, but remember to take one step at a time as you build new habits. Here are a few tips for starters.

- Keep a cloth towel handy in your kitchen and use fewer paper towels.

- Take cloth or string bags with you when you go shopping so you don't need to use paper or plastic shopping bags. Bring paper or plastic bags you have back to the store, or reuse them as long as you can. Remind yourself, until it becomes second nature. It will. Be patient with yourself.

- Start making a few substitutions for the products you usually buy. The next time that light bulb pops into a smeary gray, and it will, replace it with a compact fluorescent bulb.

- When a few substitutions become routine, add a few more.

The battery you load into your flashlight or your child's walkie-talkie contains mercury, lead, lithium, nickel, zinc, and manganese dioxide. That's right, all those toxic chemicals in that little metal tube. If your battery doesn't corrode and release its poisons while you own it, it will in a landfill, and eventually half a dozen toxic chemicals will enter our air, our soil, our water.

If you use rechargeable batteries, your battery will last longer, and rechargeable batteries are cadmium based, not mercury based. There are even solar battery chargers on the market—see Batteries, Rechargeable. Remember that batteries should be recycled with other hazardous wastes, and never throw away old car batteries. In Oregon, battery dealers must accept them for recycling.

The cleaning supplies stacked in your cupboard may be so toxic, corrosive, or flammable that many should be recycled with other hazardous wastes. When phosphates and chlorine reach our lakes and streams they can upset the balance of nature.

There are a number of nontoxic products now on the market, and we've listed them under Cleaning Supplies. Environmental action groups like the Northwest Coalition for Alternatives to Pesticides (NCAP) can provide you with safe alternatives to toxic house and garden products. It also is an excellent resource if you have poison symptoms or are considering litigation because of a poison reaction; see Environmental Action Groups.

Biodegradable and photodegradable plastic bags and diapers don't break down in our local landfills because they don't have enough air, sunlight, and water. Even those flimsy newspapers that disintegrate in Oregon rain take at least ten years to succumb in a landfill.

> *We'll all be a doubling, a doubling, a doubling. We'll all be doubling in thirty-two years.*
>
> — PETE SEEGER

Even if landfills had ideal conditions, degradable plastics would not solve the disposal problem. We don't yet know the risks to fish and wildlife that might ingest those small bits of plastic. Nor do we know the repercussions from the toxic additives and stabilizers used in the manufacturing process. Because degradable plastics cannot be recycled along with nondegradable plastic and made into sturdy products like plastic lumber, some plastic recyclers are refusing them. They can gum up the machinery in recycling plants and even cause fires.

For that reason, we've chosen to list biodegradable paper nappies or reusable cotton diapers instead of degradable diapers. According to a Greenpeace newsletter last year in this country we threw out about 18 billion disposable diapers, which added 4 million tons of debris and infectious human waste to landfills. Used disposable diapers can contain viruses and live polio vaccine residues.

If you don't want to do the actual washing, look for a diaper service in the Yellow Pages. We've listed a phone number you can call to find your nearest diaper service. There have been innovations in cloth diapers. Bumpkins has a 100 percent cotton disposable lining to go along with its one-piece, waterproof diaper. All these are listed under Diapers.

Buying paper products made from recycled paper or cotton preserves trees. It takes up to 64 percent less energy to manufacture recycled paper than virgin paper, and recycled paper produces only one-fourth the air pollution. We list everything from printing paper for stationery, envelopes, newsletters, and books to computer paper, xerographic paper, paper towels, toilet paper, and tissues under Paper, Recycled.

Recycled paper is ground up and the ink removed. Because this makes the wood fibers shorter, recycled paper isn't as strong, but it's strong enough for most uses. Obviously, 25 percent recycled is stronger than 50 percent recycled. Look at your needs before deciding which paper to buy. If you have a high-speed printer on your computer, test recycled papers before buying large quantities. Most home computer printers work well with the more-recycled paper.

Paper products are bleached during the manufacturing process, and dioxin results, in both the paper and the wastes poured into our rivers. Unbleached paper products are not quite as white, and if you must have glaring paper, there are paper products that haven't been processed with chlorine bleach. Aesthetically we prefer the softer tint. This directory, for example, is printed on recycled paper.

You might ask your printer to order the paper, or buy it yourself from the retail outlets listed under Paper, Recycled. Distributors and manufacturers will send samples. Large companies may order a variety of recycled paper products from the industrial division of distributors, or from the manufacturers directly.

Paints, solvents, strippers, and thinners all contain toxins that evaporate into the air. A 1985 Johns Hopkins University study identified more than three hundred toxic chemicals in paint.

While water-based latex paints without tetrafluoroethylene plastic are safest, they are not easy to find. Oil-based paints all contain toxic chemicals. If you want a less toxic paint product, there are some natural plant-based and wood-oil-based paints, vanishes, lacquers, and glues: see Paints and Stains, Nontoxic.

> *We could have saved it, but we were too damned cheap.*
>
> KURT VONNEGUT

Some environmental products cost a little more, but when more of us ask for them the prices will come down. Be assertive. Tell your store manager you want safer merchandise on the shelves.

Remember these three essential steps to help save Oregon. First, reduce the number of polluting substances you use. In the spring while tulips shoulder out of the ground, use an organic fertilizer. When the aphids join ranks and attack your roses, go to one of the organically committed garden stores we've listed and find a substitute for those petrochemicals. Since the use of fossil fuels is our most tenacious environmental problem, reductions must be made in our energy and gasoline consumption. Drive your car as if you paid a dollar more a gallon for gas. Get a free energy audit, then make your home as snug as possible. And the answer to that philosophical question whether a television really exists if no one is in the room to hear it blathering is yes. The proof is the electricity it consumes.

Second, reuse whatever you can. Glass, plastic, newspapers, oil, and other products you recycle don't magically disappear. That's why recycling is part of the solution, not the entire answer. If you have unrecyclable plastic bags or containers find ways to use them, and turn those carrot peelings and eggshells into compost.

Third, recycle. Using recycled paper can reduce what's added to landfills by almost 40 percent. Take your recycling habits to work. Under Recycling by Businesses we give credit to some of Oregon's largest companies for their recycling efforts. Some of their in-house programs can be applied to the smallest office.

> *We have for a long time been breaking the little laws, and the big laws are beginning to catch up with us.*
>
> A. F. COVENTRY

THE SAFEST FOOD: ORGANIC AND TRANSITIONAL

> *We see the sun, we give him something; and the moon and the earth, we give them something. We beg them to take pity on us. The sun and moon look at us, and the ground gives us food.*
>
> BLACKFOOT, CROW, 1873

Actress Meryl Streep blew the whistle on Alar, a pesticide found on many commercial apples. Suddenly our nation became concerned with the carcinogenic possibilities of pesticides. People stopped buying apples, and the apple growers made changes.

Not only pesticides but herbicides (weed killers) and chemical fertilizers poison our crops. Chemical fertilizers have been found fourteen hundred feet into the soil, and whatever is in our soil eventually seeps into our groundwater.

The United Farm Workers of America found that many farm workers picking table grapes were poisoned by pesticides. They ask that we stop buying table grapes until use of these dangerous chemicals is stopped. In California grape country the town of McFarland has a child cancer rate 800 percent above the national norm. The children's parents all worked in the vineyards before their children were born. Jimmy Cacidillo recently died of leukemia. His mother says, "I will never have another child because I'm afraid."

This concern is not limited to California. SALUD is a Southern Oregon environmental group dedicated to helping poisoned farm workers; see Environmental Action Groups.

Each year across the country fifty thousand cases of pesticide poisoning are recorded. Out of 600 pesticides registered with the Environmental Protection Agency (EPA), 496 leave residues on food. "Organic" fruits, vegetables, and grains are grown with no use of chemical pesticides at all, nor with chemical fertilizers, herbicides, or insecticides. In organic agriculture no toxic chemicals get into our food, soil, air, or water.

A food can't be called organic in this state unless it meets certain criteria. Oregon's Organic Food Law (ORS 616.406) defines what can be labeled transitional and organic. Fines go as high as fifteen thousand dollars for a violation. We can be thankful that Oregon is one of the few states to register organic growers, but this program offers neither the support nor the investigative work that is provided by Oregon Tilth.

The Oregon Tilth symbol (circular with the initials OTCOG) on foods means the growers have kept records concerning crop rotations, weed and insect management, and fertilizers and pesticides (using no petrochemicals). Each farm has scheduled inspections plus the possibility of surprise visits from a Tilth representative. Samples are taken from the soil and water and from plant tissues. Tilth is dedicated to building a vital soil filled with the microbiological life that feeds plants. Tilth also promotes legislation, mails monthly newsletters, publishes books, conducts an organic yards and gardens program, and puts on a yearly Tilth Festival; see the Produce section under Food, Organic.

Certified organic growers have kept their soil chemical-additive free for several years. While farmers are switching to organic procedures, they're considered "transitional." No chemicals have been used the year they're marked transitional, but they may have been used in the previous year. To encourage more farmers to struggle through this transitional period, it's important that we purchase transitional as well as organic foods.

If you're buying nonorganic produce you can remove some of the chemicals by washing it with a diluted biodegradable, phosphate-free detergent. Be sure to rinse thoroughly. But remember you're only removing surface chemicals.

Fred Meyer, Inc. is now using an independent scientific certification company to test samples of its produce for pesticide residues. The fruits and vegetables that have passed this inspection are marked.

We list where you can find organic produce under Food, Organic, with subsections such as Baby Food and Farmers' Markets. The availability of organic produce varies greatly across the state. Eugene consumes more such foods per capita than any other city in the country. In Eastern Oregon only a few stores carry organic produce, when it's available. We've also listed organic food distributors, to help your local grocer stock safer produce.

> *Today in the United States everybody is downwind or downstream from somebody or something else.*
>
> WILLIAM D. RUCKELSHAUS

In 1987 the Oregon State Extension Service tested seventy-five crops at different sites for pesticides. At the locations tested they discovered that more than 16 million tons of active ingredients from pesticides remain in the soil. (Inert ingredients can be just as harmful.)

Remember, organic and transitional produce doesn't always look as scrumptious as conventionally grown fruits and vegetables. But the waxy coat that makes that apple gleam is often mixed with pesticides. A natural blemish or soft spot is healthier than invisible poison.

GARDENS: GROWING ORGANIC

> *I believe a leaf of grass is no less than the journeywork of the stars.*
>
> WALT WHITMAN, *SONG OF MYSELF*

To avoid food tainted with petrochemicals, consider growing your own. You don't need a "south forty" to harvest radishes, lettuce, and spinach. Many new varieties grow well in containers, and on the patio you can display a hanging basket of cherry tomatoes or a pot of cascading squash blossoms. Community gardens often have rules about chemical use, and some are completely organic. To find the community garden nearest you call your Park Bureau or city hall.

What about that little patch of green around your home and the arsenal of chemicals that promise to kill the slugs, green the grass, and burn those dandelions? Your children probably aren't playing in sprayed farm fields, but the substances you mist or scatter on your lawn can emit toxic vapors for months.

According to the *Journal of the National Cancer Institute* children in homes where pesticides are used inside as well as in the garden have a three and a half times higher risk of leukemia. The best way to combat pests is to have healthy plants. The healthy plant has more resistance, and bothersome bugs prefer sickly vegetation.

> *Every part of this soil is sacred in the estimation of my people. Every hillside, every valley, every plain and grove, has been hallowed by some sad or happy event in days long vanished.*
> CHIEF SEATTLE, SUQUAMISH, 1853

Healthy plants sprout from good soil. Not dirt, not clay, but that crumbly, moist, rich-looking stuff. The first step toward developing it is to add compost—a mulch and soil conditioner made easily from kitchen scraps (no fat, meat, bones, or grease), dried leaves, and grass clippings. Compost loosens soil so it drains better, keeps down weeds, and evens out the soil's temperature. When you use organic fertilizers mixed with compost, the minerals are available over a longer period of time.

If you want to make your own compost, select a site in your yard that receives equal amounts of sunlight and shade, then decide if you'd rather heap the compost in an open area or enclose it in a bin. If you have no enclosure, work the materials into a dense pile.

The Metro Recycling Information Center suggests some ingenious homemade compost bins. Build a three-sided enclosure out of cinder blocks, punch holes in the sides and bottom of a garbage can, make a circle out of wooden stakes and chicken wire, or construct an open box from old lumber. We've listed garden shops where you can pay fifteen to a hundred fifty dollars for ready-made bins under Composting, Bins.

Shred the compost ingredients into small bits and add enough water to keep the heap moist, not soggy (during rainy weather you might want to cover it). To increase air circulation, turn the compost once a week. Some people push rods through the heap, then remove them, so air can pass freely. Stores listed under Composting also offer organic compost starters to help break it down.

In two or three weeks, depending on the pile's size and materials used, decomposing will have begun. When the compost is dark red, brown, or black, sift through it for decomposed material. Add this to your garden by turning no more than one pound of compost per square foot into your soil.

The biggest part of landfills, nearly 11 percent, is yard clippings. In the Portland metropolitan area 1.2 million cubic yards of yard clippings end up in landfills each year. We must stop wasting this natural material. If you don't make your own compost, buy recycled compost and find depots for your yard clippings so they can be recycled (see Recycling, Yard Debris).

There are a variety of organic fertilizers on the market—everything from bat guano, which for two thousand years has been called the king of fertilizers, to Zoo Doo, straight from the elephant house at Washington Park Zoo. Ask your garden shop to demystify these products and suggest which fertilizers will build the best soil for your specific plants.

In Portland both Dragonfly and the Northwest Garden Spot have bins of organic fertilizers and can help you combine them in the amount you need. Besides a wide variety of standard organic fertilizers to mix, Whitney Farms and Down to Earth offer fertilizers already mixed specifically for roses and flowers, fruits, bulbs, and acid-loving plants; see Soil Amendments, Organic.

A number of garden shops now sell organic seeds and organic vegetable and herb starts. We even found a few places with organically grown flower starts; see Seeds, Organic, and Nurseries, Organic Plant.

> *What is a weed? A plant whose virtues have not yet been discovered.*
> — RALPH WALDO EMERSON

To control weeds pile compost on your soil. Safer has a spot weed killer, and Ringer sells an organically safe landscape cloth.

Only .003 percent of the insecticide used in the United States actually reaches the designated insects. Insecticides are toxic to birds, algae, fish, and people as well. For years we have been bombarded with poisons. Because pesticide manufacturers supplied most of the health data on more than two hundred test-approved pesticides, we cannot be sure about long-term effects.

There are nontoxic powders, soaps, and sprays that don't kill beneficial insects, which guard your plants. We list them under Pest Control, Safe.

Not all bugs are bad guys, and you can sprinkle your garden with such beneficial organisms as ladybugs and praying mantises. *Bacillus thuringiensis* (BT) paralyzes the digestive tracts of some insects, especially leaf-eating caterpillars.

We've all watched flies cleaning themselves. Flies scrape their legs to remove life-threatening dust. Dust clogs breathing holes and removes the waxy coating on their exoskeletons, which protects them from drying out. Diatomaceous earth (made of lacy fossilized minerals) sticks fast to soft-bodied insects, and so destroys them. Scatter it around your garden border to stop snails and slugs. It's so safe farmers use it in grain to increase the health and weight of animals. It's also a good flea powder, and applied to the soil, adds trace elements. When you spot something nibbling in your garden go to your garden shop, describe the varmint, then request an organic solution.

> *We dry our wet articles and have the blankets fleed, The flees are so troublesom that I have slept but little for two nights past and we have regularly to kill them out of our blanket every day....*
>
> **GEORGE ROGERS CLARK AT FORT CLATSOP, DECEMBER 26, 1809**

There are safe pest controls for fleas, termites, cockroaches, and mice. Some chemicals used against termites have been found on household goods more than a month after fumigation. Others have been linked to nervous system damage in fumigation workers. Exterminators who specialize in organic methods are also listed under Pest Control. We include as well a list of questions provided by the Northwest Coalition for Alternatives to Pesticides (NCAP); use it as a basis of discussion with any exterminators who may bring chemicals into your home.

Ant and roach control can be simple and nontoxic. Boric acid powder is one chemical that's less toxic than others and kills both pests. We've also found a better mousetrap—one that traps the critter and, when you set it outside, allows the mouse to chew its way to freedom through a cracker barrier.

SOCIALLY RESPONSIBLE INVESTING ....

We have no more right to consume happiness without producing it than to consume wealth without producing it.
—GEORGE BERNARD SHAW, *CANDIDA*

At one time ethical investing was said to be better for your conscience than for your wallet. Times have changed. *Barron's* Lipper Gauge, February 12, 1990, compared the five-year performance of four socially responsible equity mutual funds to that of all equity mutual funds. They showed a 123.74 percent return against 116.85 percent. In the same five-year period, 1984 to 1989, monies screened for social issues rose from $25 billion to $500 billion. Ideals can have a voice on Wall Street.

Every dollar you spend or invest counts as a vote in our economic system. At the supermarket you can ask your grocer to stock environmentally smart products. In the money market you can do the same.

A system of negative and positive screening has been developed for evaluating companies. If you oppose weapons production, alcohol, South Africa, or whatever, check negative screens for what a mutual or money fund will not finance. A positive screen tells you how your money can back issues you support. We include screens wherever the information is available, under Investments, Socially Responsible.

Some funds, like the Calvert Social Investment Fund, actively support environmental safety and refuse to invest in toxic pesticides, chlorofluorocarbon (CFC) manufacture, or any company involved in environmental litigation. Each fund has its particular emphasis. Read the prospectuses, and decide which one suits you.

Our list of Oregon financial advisors is from the Social Investment Forum (SIF). Founded in 1981, the Forum includes more than five hundred investment and research professionals nationwide. SIF, an information clearinghouse, does not manage money but instead tracks the growth of socially invested funds, publishes newsletters, and sponsors conferences throughout the country. Carsten Henningsen, of Progressive Securities in Portland, is an SIF board member.

The Coalition for Environmentally Responsible Economies (or CERES, after the Roman goddess of agriculture) is a new project of SIF.

In 1989 CERES published the Valdez Principles, intended to guide corporations toward establishment of environmentally sound policies. Let's hope.

> *When people lead, the leaders will follow.*
> MOHANDAS GANDHI

You don't have to go to Wall Street to invest in a sound environmental future. Start at home. Look at your credit cards and phone lines. Where do you bank? Track the money.

We list nine credit cards and two long-distance phone plans that donate a percentage of your bill to groups like Greenpeace, the Audubon Society, and the Nature Conservancy. One or 2 percent might sound minuscule, but totaled nationwide that small percentage becomes millions, possibly billions of dollars, for lobbying and investment.

Through the latter part of the eighties we've watched the demise of the S&L industry's strength. Now commercial banks are in jeopardy. Credit unions are still legally required to comply with the needs of their constituents, and their capital remains in your local area. Some commercial banks are more committed to community reinvestment than others. Security Pacific Bank has a record of community interest in Oregon. Ask your bank for its prospectus and annual report. You might personally use only Safer insecticidal soaps but find that your bank invests heavily in Dow Chemical and Exxon.

In Oregon we have one revolving loan fund and at least two sources of venture capital that can be used to fund alternative businesses and technologies. ARABLE, the revolving loan fund, is committed to the development of organic farming in Linn, Benton, and Lane counties. The Northwest Capital Network (NCN) and Oregon Resource and Technology Development Corporation (ORTDC) provide seed capital for new entrepreneurs.

The number of socially responsible mutual funds, money-market funds, and local advisors who specialize in ethical investing is growing. We include lists of these under Investments, and also information including books, newsletters, and magazines under Publications.

getting involved ....

> *'If seven maids with seven mops*
> *Swept it for half a year,*
> *Do you suppose,' the Walrus said,*
> *'That they could get it clear?'*
> *'I doubt it,' said the Carpenter,*
> *And shed a bitter tear.*
>
> LEWIS CARROLL, *THROUGH THE LOOKING-GLASS*

Environmental groups are springing up all over Oregon. They often form out of shared passions or local abuses—the destruction of wetlands, the poisoning of farm workers, the disappearance of eagles. Many of Oregon's environmental laws have been drafted by these groups.

Some groups, like the Audubon Society, have chapters throughout the state; others such as Lawnchairs for Peace aren't cited in the phone book. We list only a portion of these organizations, but we discovered a group, The Environmental Communications Network, that is compiling a computer data base of every environmental organization in the state. Call them—see the listing under Environmental Action Groups—and they will research organizations close to you that have a similar environmental concern.

Be an assertive consumer. Besides requesting environmental products write and complain to companies that contribute to environmental problems. Support the companies who support our environment. Tuna fish caught without harming dolphins is now in supermarkets because consumers and environmentalists took action. The three biggest tuna canners in the United States recently changed their fishing practices because of consumer pressure. Fred Meyer, Inc. was a leader in this area.

Make sure you're registered to vote in the next election. The Oregon League of Conservation Voters (OLCV) rates and publishes the environmental records of most candidates and will gladly send you this information. If you're unhappy with a political environmental stand, write your public officials. We list their addresses under Elected Officials to Lobby. If you support a candidate's position consider a donation, or volunteer time to ensure that he or she is elected.

> *Everyone needs beauty as well as bread, places to lay in and pray in where nature may heal and cheer and give strength to body and soul alike.*
>
> JOHN MUIR

Not all environmental changes involve doing something different or buying something new. It's not as simple as changing our buying-for-convenience reflex. We need to change the way we perceive ourselves and our planet. Even if we don't survive, our planet will. The earth does not need us, we need the earth.

The actions we choose must be based not on what's quickest, what's easiest, what's cheapest, but on what will ensure a living earth for the next generation. If one generation's greed jeopardizes the resources of another generation, our legacy is a vandalized world.

> *Your time of decay may be distant, but it will surely come, for even the white man whose God walked and talked with him as friend with friend, cannot be exempt from the common destiny. We may be brothers after all.*
>
> CHIEF SEATTLE, SUQUAMISH, 1853

Besides seeing our destinies linked with those of our children, our grandchildren, and our great grandchildren, we must recognize the web encompassing ourselves and all living things. We may not see the bloated fish floating on dioxin-laced water, but when we buy bleached paper we are assuring that more fish will die.

We cannot measure a plant or animal's right to existence in dollars and cents. Is eliminating a species any less immoral than destroying a Rembrandt? Something precious has been lost forever. When a species dies, a flaw has occurred in its ecosystem. That vanishing animal or plant is like the canary that miners used to take into mines. Miners knew if the canary died there was a gas buildup, and they were warned.

We also have been warned.

part two
OUTLETS AND SOURCES

Automobile Products

ANTIFREEZE

Solar Electric
116 Fourth St., Santa Rosa, CA 95401
(800) 832-1986, (707) 542-1900
Fax (707) 542-4358

Not all antifreeze is dangerous to the environment. Solar Electric offers an engine coolant and antifreeze made with propylene glycol instead of ethylene glycol. Biodegradable and nonhazardous, it can protect your car and the environment for $11 a gallon.

SMOG REDUCTION

E.M.A. (Environmental Marketing Association)
P.O. Box 70, Ojai, CA 93024
(805) 646-4647

The MHD Kynetik Fuel Conditioner is a magnetic unit that attaches to your car's fuel line. The manufacturer claims that it alters the magnetic charge of hydrogen molecules, causing fuel to burn cleaner. It never needs changing, and it's also claimed to provide 25 percent better mileage; $99 for four-cylinder engines, $149 for six- or eight-cylinder engines.

Inspection Systems Engineering, Inc.
American Pacific Co.
7 Whatney St. #200, Irvine, CA 92718
(714) 583-7191

While you drive, the air you breathe inside your car is filled with irritating gases, toxic hydrocarbons, and dust. Your car can become a moving air cleaner with the Filt-Aire Activated Carbon Filter, which absorbs many air pollutants. It costs about $10 and lasts about five thousand miles. Call the manufacturer to see if there's a distributor close to you.

MAIL ORDER:

EcoSource
51 Mill Station Rd., Bldg. E, Sebastopol, CA 95472
(800) 688-8345

EcoSource sells a device named Vitalizer which it claims works much like the MHD Kynetik Fuel Conditioner. Testing on a 1985 Subaru four-wheel-drive wagon, the company claims an 88.5 percent reduction of hydrocarbon emissions and no carbon monoxide emitted, with 19.5 percent better mileage; $129.95 for four-, six-, and eight-cylinder engines; $499.95 for diesel trucks. There's a thirty-day money-back guarantee.

Ecosource also sells the Frantz Filter, which it claims eliminates the need to change oil. The filter must be changed every two thousand to three thousand miles and a fresh quart of oil added to replace that absorbed by the filter. It costs $159 for domestic autos, $164 for foreign makes; also, $4 for a replacement filter, $37 for a full-flow adapter. Certain foreign makes need an additional adapter. For technical assistance call (209) 466-0103 and identify yourself as an EcoSource customer.

Solar Electric
116 Fourth St., Santa Rosa, CA 95401
(800) 832-1986, (707) 542-1900
Fax (707) 542-4358

If you can't afford an electric car right now, Solar Electric offers the Vitalizer for gasoline-driven cars, estimating it provides an increase in mileage from 5 to 20 percent and reduction in exhaust hydrocarbons and carbon monoxide by 80 percent. The Vitalizer costs $129.95 for four-, six-, and eight-cylinder engines, $499.95 for diesel trucks, and can pay for itself in as little as six months. It comes with a ten-year warranty and a thirty-day money-back guarantee.

*a*UTOMOBILES AND SCOOTERS, ENERGY EFFICIENT

The most energy-efficient cars get from 35 to 40 mpg and are a light color with tinted glass—to stay cooler in warm weather and reduce air-conditioning needs. The following cars were rated by the Environmental Protection Agency's 1989 *Gas Mileage Guide* as getting 34 or more mpg for city driving (highway driving gets better mileage, of course). All cars listed here are subcompacts. Whether or not you decide to buy one of these cars, consider gas mileage when you make your next purchase.

Avoid gas guzzlers—new cars that get fewer than 22 mpg—and remember that such options as power windows add weight and lower fuel efficiency. Radial tires can improve fuel efficiency by 4 percent.

The Ten Most Energy Efficient Cars

	MPG CITY	MPG HIGHWAY
Geo Metro (manual) Chevrolet	53	58
Honda Civic CRX HF (manual)	50	56
Ford Festiva (manual)	39	43
Daihatsu Charade (manual)	38	42
Geo Metro LSi (automatic)	38	40
Isuzu I-Mark (manual)	37	41
Toyota Tercel (manual)	35	41
Honda Civic (manual)	34	38
Subaru Justy (manual)	34	37
Subaru Justy (automatic)	34	35

If Not Now...When?
512 N.W. Twenty-first Ave., Portland, OR 97209
222-4471
This Portland environmental store has on display a solar moped, designed for the streets of London by Cleve Sinclaire. It comes with a battery recharger or optional solar panel. The moped travels one thousand miles for the price of one gallon of gas.

Electric Motor Car Co.
116 Fourth St., Santa Rosa, CA 95401
(800) 832-1986, (707) 542-1900
Fax (707) 542-4358
Yes, you can get an electric car now. This company offers a four-passenger sedan for $15,000; a step-van for $12,500; a top-of-the-line sports car for $28,000; or an electric scooter for just $1,000. The cars can go fifty miles before they need recharging, and you can recharge them with solar cells or by plugging them into a household socket with an extension cord.

*b*AGS

See also RECYCLED PRODUCTS

COTTON SHOPPING BAGS

Sturdy cotton bags for shopping are popping up all over, even in supermarkets. They vary in size from string bags that fold to fit in a pocket or glove compartment to canvas bags in grocery-hauling size. If you can't find what you like at your supermarket, here are some smaller, environmentally oriented stores that stock them.

WILLAMETTE VALLEY

First Alternative
1007 S.E. Third Ave., Corvallis, OR 97333
753-3115
Bags of varying sizes and prices.

Sunshine General Store
824 W. Main St., Cottage Grove, OR 97424
942-8836
Varying sizes; prices $1.50 to $8.

Down to Earth Home Shop
Fifth Ave. & Olive St., Eugene, OR 97401
344-6357
Bags for $2.95 to $8.95.

Friendly Foods and Deli
2757 Friendly St., Eugene, OR 97405
683-2079
An assortment of bag sizes and prices—$1 to $8.49.

Kiva
125 W. Eleventh Ave., Eugene, OR 97401
342-8666
Bags for $14 to $22.

New Frontier Market
Eighth Ave. & Van Buren St., Eugene, OR 97502
345-7401
Bags for $6 to $12.

Oasis
2489 Willamette St., Eugene, OR 97405
345-1014
Mesh for $3.50, canvas, $11.95. Oasis pays $.05 for each returned grocery bag.

Red Barn Grocery
357-A Van Buren St., Eugene, OR 97402
342-7503
Small bags only, from $1 to $2.

Sundance
748 E. Twenty-fourth Ave., Eugene, OR 97401
345-0141
A wide selection, from $5.95 to $12.

Daily Grind
4026 S.E. Hawthorne Blvd., Portland, OR 97214
223-5521
Bags for $7.95.

Earth Mercantile
6344 S.W. Capitol Hwy., Portland, OR 97201
246-4935
String bags, $4.95; large canvas bags, $18.

Ecology House
341 S.W. Morrison St., Portland, OR 97204
223-4883
Bags for $6.50 to $25.

Food Front Co-op Grocery
2375 N.W. Thurman St., Portland, OR 97210
222-5658
Cloth bags from $7.75 to $10. Also the store gives $.05 for each returned grocery bag and has bins for customers to recycle brown paper, cardboard, and glass.

Happy Harvest Grocery
2348 S.E. Ankeny St., Portland, OR 97214
235-5358
Bags for $6 to $15.

If Not Now...When?
512 N.W. Twenty-first Ave., Portland, OR 97209
222-4471
Bags for $10.

The Nature Company
700 S.W. Fifth Ave., Portland, OR 97204
222-0015
Bags for $4.95.

Nature's Fresh Northwest
5909 S.W. Corbett St., Portland, OR 97219
244-3934
All four stores have string bags, $6.95; large canvas bags, $9.95.

3449 N.E. Twenty-fourth Ave., Portland, OR 97212
288-3414

6344 S.W. Capitol Hwy., Portland, OR 97225
244-3110
This Nature's store also has bins for recycling plastic (the recycling label must indicate 2, 4, or 6). Customers can recycle a bag full on each visit. Eventually all the Nature's stores will have plastic recycling bins.

4000 S.W. 117th Ave., Beaverton, OR 97005
646-3824

People's Food Store
3029 S.E. Twenty-first Ave., Portland, OR 97214
232-9051
For three different sizes, from coffee sack to grocery bag size, prices range from $1.95 to $8.

Heliotrope Natural Foods
2060 Market St. N.E., Salem, OR 97301
362-5487
Bags for $9 to $15. Heliotrope gives $.05 back on large grocery bags and will recycle any plastic that comes from the store.

SOUTHERN OREGON
Ashland Community Food Store
37 Third Ave., Ashland, OR 97520
482-2237
Coffee and flour bags for $1 and canvas grocery bags for $7.95.

Harmony Natural Store
116 Main St., Rogue River, OR 97537
582-3075
Mesh string bags for $4.95 and large cloth bags for $8.95.

New Day Quality Groceries
210 S.E. Jackson St., Roseburg, OR 97470
672-0275
Bags for $7.95 to $8.95.

EASTERN AND CENTRAL OREGON

Good Food Store
1124 N.W. Newport Ave., Bend, OR 97702
389-6533
Bags for about $10.

Nature's General Store
Wagner Mall, Bend, OR 97702
382-6732
Canvas grocery bags are $9.50; all proceeds are donated to an action group against cruel animal testing.

Wy' East General Store
110 Eighth Ave., Hood River, OR 97031
386-6181
Bags for $5 to $15.

Oregon Natural Market
340 S.W. Fifth Ave., Ontario, OR 97914
889-8714
Bags for $8.95.

Cornucopia General Store
Wagner Square, Redmond, OR 97756
548-5911
String bags, $3.25.

Apple Jack's
110 S. Spruce St., Sisters, OR 97759

549-5781
Mesh bags are $4.50 and canvas bags are $5.99.

THE COAST
The Community Store, Inc.
1389 Duane St., Astoria, OR 97103
325-0027
Mesh bags are $7.30 and canvas bags are $11.

Osburn's Grocery & Deli
240 N. Hemlock St., Cannon Beach, OR 97110
436-2234
Bags for $12.95 to $13.95.

Nosler's Natural Grocery
99 E. First St., Coquille, OR 97423
396-4823
Bags for $10.95.

Trillium Natural Grocery
1026 S.E. Jetty Ave., Lincoln City, OR 97367
994-5665
Mesh produce bags are $5.95 and canvas bags are $6.99.

Oceana Co-op Natural Foods
415 N.W. Coast St., Newport, OR 97365
265-8285
Mesh bags, $6.

Coos Head Food Store
1960 Sherman Ave., North Bend, OR 97459
756-7264
Bags are sometimes stocked.

Grady's Market
580 N.E. Broadway St., Waldport, OR 97394
563-3542
Bags for $5.99.

MAIL ORDER:
EcoSource
9051 Mill Station Rd., Bldg. E, Sebastopol, CA 95472
(800) 688-8345
Canvas bags in various weights and sizes—many with colorful designs—are $10 to $25. Unbleached cotton drawstring bags in four sizes are $1.25 to $1.75; $16.50 for a set with four in each size. Also string bags: four six-ounce bags for $16.95 or two three-ounce bags for $8.95.

Real Goods
966 Mazzoni St., Ukiah, CA 95482
(800) 762-7325
Heavy-construction cotton string bags, made in the United States with soft cotton handles; $5 each.

Seventh Generation
Colchester, VT 05446-1672
(800) 456-1177
Cotton string bags, two for $8.95 and four for $16.95.

Solar Electric
116 Fourth St., Santa Rosa, CA 95401
(800) 832-1986, (707) 542-1900
Fax (707) 542-4358
Canvas shopping bags, one for $8.95 and three for $23.95. Reusable lunch sacks, one for $6.95 and three for $18.95. Cotton string bags, two for $8.95, four for $16.95.

PAPER TRASH BAGS

Here's the alternative to plastic trash bags. They are strong and decompose in landfills.
Earth Mercantile
6344 S.W. Capitol Hwy., Portland, OR 97201
246-4935

MAIL ORDER:
EcoSource
9051 Mill Station Rd., Bldg. E, Sebastopol, CA 95472
(800) 688-8345

Refuse bags of recycled paper; fifteen-bag packs in thirty-gallon size are $9.95.

Seventh Generation
Colchester, VT 05446-1672
(800) 456-1177
Biodegradable paper bags for trash, twenty in each package: thirty-gallon size, $9.95; thirteen-gallon, $7.95; eight-gallon, $5.95; or one package of each size for $21.95.

Smith and Hawken
25 Corte Madera, Mill Valley, CA 94941
(415) 383-2000
Biodegradable thirty-gallon paper bags for trash; $8 for ten bags.

Walnut Acres
Penns Creek, PA 17862
(800) 433-3998
Biodegradable paper trash bags in twenty-bag packages; nine-gallon size, $9.95; thirteen-gallon, $11.95; and thirty-gallon, $16.95.

SANDWICH-BAG SUBSTITUTES

Tupperware
(800) 858-7221
Instead of buying plastic throwaway sandwich bags, why not use sandwich boxes? Tupperware makes bread-shape sandwich boxes in just the right size with tight-fitting lids that don't pop off; four for $7.20. Call for the distributor nearest you.

BATTERIES

See also THE SECTION ON RECYCLING BATTERIES

CODE RED BATTERIES

If batteries are stored for a long time, they may not be good when you need them. The Code Red battery will last for twenty years. It isn't activated until you rotate the top. It comes in size D only.

MAIL ORDER:
Real Goods
966 Mazzoni St., Ukiah, CA 95482
(800) 762-7325
Along with every other conceivable kind of battery, this mail-order house also has Code Reds.

MANUFACTURER:
Energetics Corp.
P.O. Box 2320, Redmond, WA 98073
(206) 881-1144

RECHARGEABLE BATTERIES

Household batteries for your flashlight, radio, camera, and toys contain such heavy metals as mercury and cadmium. The fewer batteries used, the less toxic metal finds its way into landfills and hazardous dumps. Rechargeable cadmium batteries can be used over and over. And when you're finished with them, take them to a hazardous waste pickup point, please. Many stores now sell rechargeable batteries, along with battery chargers.

STATEWIDE

Ace Hardware Stores
Battery chargers and different-size batteries.

Coast to Coast
Rechargers and AAA, AA, C, D, and nine-volt rechargeable batteries.

Fred Meyer, Inc.
The Photo/Sound Departments carry rechargers and rechargeable batteries in every size.

Pay 'N Pack
Rechargers and batteries in most sizes.

Radio Shack
Rechargers and nickel-cadmium batteries.

True Value Hardware
Rechargers and batteries in all sizes.

WILLAMETTE VALLEY
Oasis
2489 Willamette St., Eugene, OR 97405
345-1014
Rechargers and several sizes of batteries.

Builder's Square
1160 N. Hayden Meadows Dr., Portland, OR 97217
286-0074
Both stores have rechargers for AA, C, and D batteries.

2315 S.E. Eighty-second Ave., Portland, OR 97215
775-0040

Earth Mercantile
6344 S.W. Capitol Hwy., Portland, OR 97201
246-4935
Solar battery chargers and AA, C, and D batteries.

Ecology House
341 S.W. Morrison St., Portland, OR 97204
223-4883
Rechargers and Dynacharge batteries.

If Not Now...When?
512 N.W. Twenty-first Ave., Portland, OR 97201
222-4471
Solar rechargers and batteries in a variety of sizes.

MAIL ORDER:
Co-op America
c/o Order Service
10 Farrell St., South Burlington, VT 05403
(800) 456-1177

Panasonic nickel-cadmium batteries can be recharged up to five hundred times. AA batteries are six for $5 and C or D sizes are four for $8. A solar battery charger that takes one or two days to recharge four to six batteries, performance guaranteed, is $26.50. Nonmembers pay an extra $3.50 service charge per order; annual membership, $15 per year.

EcoSource
9051 Mill Station Rd., Bldg. E, Sebastopol, CA 95472
(800) 688-8345
For $29.95 you can buy a metered solar charger for nickel-cadmium batteries that can charge four AAs and two Cs or Ds. A pocket-size solar charger for AAs is $13.95; the AA batteries are $2.50 each; C and D size, $4.50 each.

Real Goods
966 Mazzoni St., Ukiah, CA 95482
(800) 762-7325
In addition to battery chargers that are solar-powered or that recharge from a twelve-volt power source (such as your car), the catalog has a solar button charger designed for the mercury button-type batteries used in watches, hearing aids, and calculators; $15. It also sells Code Red batteries (D cell only).

Seventh Generation
Colchester, VT 05446-1672
(800) 456-1177
The rechargeable batteries are designed for industrial use and can be recharged up to five hundred times. They are sold in pairs: AA is $5.95, C is $14.95, and D is $24.95.

BENEFICIAL ORGANISMS, *see* **PEST CONTROL**

BOTTLES, BEER, *see* **RECYCLED PRODUCTS**

BUILDING MATERIALS, *see* **RECYCLED PRODUCTS**

BUMPERS, *see* **RECYCLED PRODUCTS**

CAR WASH, *see* **WATER CONSERVATION PRODUCTS**

CLEANING SUPPLIES

Many household cleaners are made from petroleum by-products and chemicals that are better kept out of our water and sewage systems. Phosphates, which are added to soften water and help the cleaning agents work, also have a negative effect on aquatic life. Alternative cleaning products that are made from vegetable material and do not harm waters or aquatic life are now available. These products are great and will make your home smell like citrus instead of a gas station rest room. For everything you need to know about nontoxic cleaning supplies see *Clean and Green*, listed immediately below.

Our favorite cleaner is Bi-O-Kleen. Since it releases no biotoxins and degrades in six to twenty-four hours, it can be used as gray water on plants. Bi-O-Kleen is a produce wash, detergent, carpet cleaner, pet shampoo, and bathroom and shower cleaner. Think of all that saved packaging.

If none of these stores is near you, look in your local supermarket for one of the mild, all-time-favorite soaps: Ivory Snow, Fels Naptha, Arm & Hammer, or Bon Ami. Or use one of the mail-order sources at the end of this section. Phosphate detergents have been banned in the Portland area and are no longer available at any Fred Meyer store.

Clean and Green, by Annie Berthold Bond
Woodstock, Ceres Press: 1990. $6.45. Available in bookstores and from:
Ceres Press
P.O. Box 87, Woodstock, NY 12498
(914) 679-5573

WILLAMETTE VALLEY

First Alternative
1007 S.E. Third Ave., Corvallis, OR 97333
753-3115
Bi-O-Kleen plus Ecover and Life Tree products.

Sunshine General Store
824 W. Main St., Cottage Grove, OR 97424
942-8836
Soaps and cleaning products from Ecover, Country Safe, and Applegate.

Down to Earth Home Store
Fifth Ave. & Olive St., Eugene, OR 97401
344-6357
Down to Earth has a citrus-based solvent, Citra-Solv, that dissolves everything from gum to grease and can be used as an air deodorizer. Liquid Life Forms, a safe drain cleaner, acts as a bacterial digestant and deodorant. The store also carries Life Tree and Seventh Generation cleaning products.

Friendly Foods and Deli
2757 Friendly St., Eugene, OR 97405
683-2079
Bi-O-Kleen and the full lines of Life Tree, Ecover, New Age, and Lifeline, plus Citra-Solv.

Kiva
125 W. Eleventh Ave., Eugene, OR 97401
342-8666
Applegate laundry detergent and the Country Safe cleaning products.

New Frontier Market
Eighth Ave. & Van Buren St., Eugene, OR 97502
345-7401
All-purpose Bi-O-Kleen.

Oasis
2489 Willamette St., Eugene, OR 97405
345-1014
Oasis carries not only every imaginable cleaning product but five or six different brands.

Red Barn Grocery
357-A Van Buren St., Eugene, OR 97402
342-7503
The grocery has Bi-O-Kleen and the complete line of cleaning products and soaps from Life Tree, Ecover, Planet, Infinity, New Age, and Earth Rite. For dishwashers it highly recommends Kleer. This seems expensive, but since one-eighth teaspoon is all you need, a box should last a year.

Sundance
748 E. Twenty-fourth Ave., Eugene, OR 97401
345-0141
Bi-O-Kleen plus products from Ecover, Lifeline, New Age, and Country Safe.

Daily Grind
4026 S.E. Hawthorne Blvd., Portland, OR 97214
223-5521
Bi-O-Kleen, plus cleaning products and soaps by Life Tree and Planet.

Earth Mercantile
6344 S.W. Capitol Hwy., Portland, OR 97201
246-4935
From Kleer the store stocks a chlorine-free bleach, dishwashing soap, and Glass Mate, an all-purpose cleaner without ammonia or phosphate. It also carries Ecover and Country Safe cleaners and soaps.

Food Front Co-op Grocery
2375 N.W. Thurman St., Portland, OR 97210
222-5658
Bi-O-Kleen plus products from Life Tree, Lifeline, Ecover, and Country Safe, and old-time Bon Ami.

Happy Harvest Grocery
2348 S.E. Ankeny St., Portland, OR 97214
235-5358
Kleer automatic dishwashing soap plus Life Tree, Ecover, and Country Safe cleaning and detergent products.

If Not Now...When?
512 N.W. Twenty-first Ave., Portland, OR 97209
222-4471
The complete lines of cleaning and soap products from New Age, Life Tree, and Safer.

Nature's Fresh Northwest
5909 S.W. Corbett St., Portland, OR 97219
244-3934
All four stores have Bi-O-Kleen and the Ecover line.

6344 S.W. Capitol Hwy., Portland, OR 97225
244-3110

3449 N.E. Twenty-fourth Ave., Portland, OR 97212
288-3414

4000 S.W. 117th Ave., Beaverton, OR 97005
646-3824

People's Food Store
3029 S.E. Twenty-first Ave., Portland, OR 97214

232-9051
All-purpose Bi-O-Kleen plus Bon Ami, Cottage, Tree Life, and Ecover products.

Heliotrope Natural Foods
2060 Market N.E., Salem, OR 97301
362-5487
Bi-O-Kleen plus safe dishwashing liquids, detergents, and hand soaps.

Perrywinkle Provisions
1101 Main St., Sweet Home, OR 97386
367-6614
Bi-O-Kleen plus products from Ecover and Life Tree.

SOUTHERN OREGON

Ashland Community Food Store
37 Third St., Ashland, OR 97520
482-2237
The entire lines from Ecover and Life Tree.

Promise Natural Food Store
503 S. Main St., Canyonville, OR 97417
839-4167
Ecover's floor cleaner, toilet cleaners, and detergent, and from Country Safe, laundry soap.

Hammer's Model Market
202 S. Redwood Hwy., Cave Junction, OR 97523
592-3236
Toilet cleaners, detergents, tile and floor cleaners, and dishwashing soap from Life Tree, New Age, and Country Safe.

New Life Natural Foods
202 W. Lister St., Cave Junction, OR 97523
592-3816
Dr. Bronner's, New Age, and Ecover products.

Harmony Natural Store
116 Main St., Rogue River, OR 97537
582-3075

The store is now expanding its Ecover line and can special-order anything from Life Tree.

New Day Quality Groceries
210 S.E. Jackson St., Roseburg, OR 97470
627-0275
Ecover cleaning products.

EASTERN AND CENTRAL OREGON

Nature's General Store
Wagner Mall, Bend, OR 97702
382-6732
Cleaning products from the Ecover line.

Wy' East
110 Eighth St., Hood River, OR 97031
386-6181
Cleaning and detergent products from Country Life.

Nature's Pantry Natural Food Store
1907 Fourth St., La Grande, OR 97850
963-7955
Golden Lotus dishwashing and other soaps.

Oregon Natural Market
340 S.W. Fifth St., Ontario, OR 97914
889-8714
A few safe cleaning products.

Cornucopia General Store
Wagner Square, Redmond, OR 97756
523-6281
Earth Rite dishwashing soap, laundry soap, and wood cleaner.

THE COAST

The Community Store, Inc.
1389 Duane St., Astoria, OR 97103
325-0027
Bi-O-Kleen plus Dr Bronner's dishwashing soap and detergent.

Generous Helpings
604 Spruce St., Brookings, OR 97415
469-5414
Life Tree and a few other brands.

Osburn's Grocery & Deli
240 N. Hemlock St., Cannon Beach, OR 97110
436-2234
The store will order safe products on request.

Nosler's Natural Grocery
99 E. First St., Coquille, OR 97423
396-4823
The Ecover and Life Tree lines.

Trillium Natural Grocery
1026 S.E. Jetty Ave., Lincoln City, OR 97367
994-5665
Good old Bon Ami.

Oceana Co-op Natural Foods
415 N.W. Coast St., Newport, OR 97365
265-8285
Lifeline products.

Coos Head Food Store
1960 Sherman Ave., North Bend, OR 97459
756-7264
Bi-O-Kleen plus Ecover products.

Grady's Market
580 N.E. Broadway, Waldport, OR 97394
563-3542
A variety of safe cleaning products.

MAIL ORDER:
Baubiologie "Healthful" Hardware
207B Sixteenth St., Pacific Grove, CA 93950
(408) 372-8626
Products from Allens, Granny's Old Fashioned, Golden Lotus, and

AFM Enterprises (including carpet guard, wax and polish for floors and cars, floor sealer, and mildew cleaner).

Co-op America
c/o Order Service
10 Farrell St., South Burlington, VT 05403
(800) 456-1177
Ecover products, including a toilet cleaner, nonabrasive soft scrubbing cream for tiles, all-purpose cleaner, and dishwashing and laundry detergents. Nonmembers pay an extra $3.50 service charge per order; annual membership, $15 per year.

EcoSource
9051 Mill Station Rd., Bldg. E, Sebastopol, CA 95472
(800) 688-8345
EcoSource's cleaning products have a money-back guarantee and are free of all phosphates, alcohol, dye, preservatives, and petroleum by-products. They include an all-purpose cleaner, dishwashing detergent, body soap, spot remover, glass and tile cleaners, and a chlorine-free bleach safe for septic systems. EcoSource carries Oasis laundry detergent, which biodegrades and is safe for plants.

E.M.A.(Environmental Marketing Association)
P.O. Box 70, Ojai, CA 93024
(805) 646-4647
PuriSol cleaning solution was found effective in controlling mold, fungus, and mildew growing on fruits and vegetables at the University of California at Davis. It eliminates odors in pet bedding, litter boxes, and rest rooms and removes contaminants from produce, counter tops, and carpets. You can even use it on minor cuts and abrasions!

Jerrick
18149 Ventura Blvd. #149, Tarzana, CA 91356
(818) 344-5214
Jerrick carries a variety of products that are biodegradable and recycled products that have been tested without animal cruelty, including toilet and glass cleaners and dish and laundry detergents.

Jim Guasti Plumbing Service
4102 Orange Ave. #107-72, Long Beach, CA 90807

(213) 424-3315

An ecologically knowledgeable plumber, Jim Guasti is your only mail-order source for Bio-Plus and Bio-Safe cleaners. Made of the same bacteria used by sewage treatment plants, Bio-Plus can be used as a laundry presoak, added to carpet cleaner, and used for many other purposes. Bio-Safe replaces caustic drain cleaners that pollute the water and destroy good bacteria.

Nigra Enterprises
5699 Kanan Rd., Agoura, CA 91301
(818) 889-6877

Jim Nigra is a consultant and broker for products for people with environmental sensitivities. Many of the excellent environmentally safe products he sells will clean up your indoor environment, including AFM Enterprises cleaning and sealing products.

Plant Chemistry
1365 Rufina Circle, Santa Fe, NM 87501
(800) 621-2591

Nontoxic soaps, shoe polish (clear, brown, and black), and furniture polish.

Real Goods
966 Mazzoni St., Ukiah, CA 95482
(800) 762-7325

Nontoxic household cleaners including biodegradable liquid beeswax, shoe polish, spot remover, and laundry detergent.

Seventh Generation
Colchester, VT 05446-1672
(800) 456-1177

Seventh Generation carries its own nontoxic and biodegradable cleaners, guaranteed to do the job or your money back. Many are triple concentrated, so a little goes a long way. The products include laundry liquid and powder, nonchlorine bleach, clothes softener, dishwashing liquid and powder, wool washer, floor soap for wood or linoleum, glass cleaner, and toilet cleaner, as well as cellulose sponges.

Terra Verde Products
P.O. Box 1353, Clifton, CO 81520

(No phone)
The Winter White brand of laundry and home-care products are phosphate free and biodegradable, and they include prewash solution, nonchlorine bleach, laundry detergent, dishwashing detergent, glass cleaner, and all-purpose cleaner. No animals were used for testing these products and no animal by-products are contained in them.

Walnut Acres
Penns Creek, PA 17862
(800) 433-3998
Walnut Acres carries the Ecover line of cleaners, including a cream cleaner, dishwashing liquid, floor cleaner, laundry detergent, toilet-bowl cleaner, fabric softener, and wool wash.

CODE RED BATTERIES, see BATTERIES

COMPACT FLUORESCENT LIGHT BULBS, see LIGHT BULBS

COMPOST, see SOIL AMENDMENTS, ORGANIC

COMPOSTING

BINS

STATEWIDE
Fred Meyer, Inc.
Each year this chain carries several different kinds of bins. It also gives out free pamphlets on how to make your own.

WILLAMETTE VALLEY
Vollstedt's Green Thumb
410 Pacific Blvd. S.W., Albany, OR 97321
928-2521
Bins for $20.

Garland Nursery
5470 N.E. Hwy. 20, Corvallis, OR 97330
753-6601
Bins for $22 to $115.

Down to Earth Farm and Garden
Fifth Ave. & Olive St., Eugene, OR 97402
342-6820
Bins for $40 to $100.

Gray's Garden Shop
737 W. Sixth Ave., Eugene, OR 97402
345-1569
At both shops, bins for $19.95 to $119.95.

444 E. Main St., Springfield, OR 97478
747-2301

Oregon Garden Store
333 S. State St., Lake Oswego, OR 97034
697-3635
Bins for $36 to $140.

Dennis' 7 Dees
6025 S.E. Powell Blvd., Portland, OR 97206
777-1422
At all three stores, bins for $25.95 to $125.

10445 S.W. Barnes Rd., Portland, OR 97225
297-1058

1090 McVey Ave., Lake Oswego, OR 97034
636-4660

Dragonfly Gardens
2230 S.E. Hawthorne Blvd., Portland, OR 97202
235-9150
Bins for $14.95 to $120.

Drake's 7 Dees
16519 S.E. Stark St., Portland, OR 97233
255-9225
Bins for $39 to $109.95.

Portland Nursery
5050 S.E. Stark St., Portland, OR 97215
231-5050
Bins for $24.99 to $119.

SOUTHERN OREGON

Ray's Garden Center
2265 Hwy. 66, Ashland, OR 97520
482-9561
Bins for $39.99 to $149.99.

Chet's Garden Center
229 S.W. H St., Grants Pass, OR 97526
476-4424
A wide variety and price range of bins.

Redwood Nursery
1290 Redwood Ave., Grants Pass, OR 97527
476-2642
A wide variety and price range of bins.

Radford's Altamont Nursery
3237 Maryland Ave., Klamath Falls, OR 97603
884-0669
Bins are available by special order.

EASTERN AND CENTRAL OREGON

Landsystems
21336 Hwy. 20 E., Bend, OR 97701
389-5926
Bins for $25 to $100.

Redmond's Greenhouse
4101 S. Hwy. 97, Redmond, OR 97756
548-5418
Bins are available by special order.

THE COAST

Raintree Garden and Gift
Hamlet Rt., Box 304, Seaside, OR 97138

738-6980
A wide variety and price range of bins.

MAIL ORDER:
BioBin
8407 Lightmoor Ct., Bainbridge, WA 98110
(206) 842-6641
A fourteen-bushel, hexagonal compost bin made from recycled cedar is only $43, including shipping.

Gardener's Supply
128 Intervale Rd., Burlington, VT 05401
(802) 863-1700
Here find three kinds of compost bins: the square plastic Soilsaver, for $99.95; a barrel-type tumbler that you spin every day to mix the contents, for $99.95; and a square PVC-coated steel-wire bin for $39.95 that you can use with plastic liners (three for $10.95).

Gardens Alive!
Natural Gardening Research Center
Hwy. 48, Box 149, Sunman, IN 47041
(812) 623-3800
This company builds a twelve-cubic-foot bin that is thirty-one inches high and twenty-eight inches wide. Lift up the top to throw in kitchen wastes and raise the bottom slats to remove the finished compost; costs $110.

Peaceful Valley Farm Supply
P.O. Box 2209, Grass Valley, CA 95945
(916) 272-4769
The square plastic Soilsaver bin costs $105, including delivery.

Ringer
9959 Valley View Rd., Eden Prairie, MN 55344-3585
(800) 654-1047
A variety of bins, from a wire compost bin for $35 to an insulated plastic compost bin that holds up to thirteen bushels for $160.

Smith and Hawken
25 Corte Madera, Mill Valley, CA 94941

(415) 383-2000
A polyethylene compost bin (twenty-eight by twenty-eight by thirty-one inches), with detachable lid and sliding door at the bottom for easy compost removal, costs $98.

Territorial Seed Company
P.O. Box 157, Cottage, OR 97424
942-9547
An easily expandable compost bin made of four two-by-three foot galvanized panels costs $129.

INFORMATION

Agri/Home Planning
5244 Strohm Ave., North Hollywood, CA 91601
(818) 509-8131
Jim Helliwell teaches what you need to know about composting and helps folks turn incinerators into compost bins.

Common Ground Garden Program
2615 S. Grand Ave. #400, Los Angeles, CA 90007
(213) 744-4341
Common Ground will send you free information on how to compost and how to build your own bin.

Eco-Home
4344 Russell Ave., Los Angeles, CA 90027
(213) 662-5207
For $3 Eco-Home will send you a composting information packet that includes compost bin designs and a rapid composting method for impatient gardeners like us.

John Inskeep Environmental Learning Center (ELC)
Clackamas Community College
19600 S. Molalla Ave., Oregon City, OR 97045
657-6958, x351 or x457
ELC gives a $3 Rapid Composting Seminar at the college.

Let It Rot, by Stu Campbell
Pawnal, Vermont: Garden Way, 1975. $5.95. Available at book-

stores or from:
Garden Way Publications
c/o Storey Communications
Schoolhouse Rd., Pawnal, VT 05261
(802) 823-5811
or from:
Armstrong's The Home and Garden Place
11321 W. Pico Blvd., West Los Angeles, CA 90064
(213) 477-8023
This book tells you everything you wanted to know about what goes into compost and how to make it, and includes bin designs.

Metro Recycling Information Center
2000 S.W. First Ave., Portland, OR 97201-5398
224-5555
A twenty-two-page free recycling pamphlet called *The Art of Composting* is offered Oregon residents living in the Metro area. Metro will mail this information to you, or you can pick it up at the office.

Santa Monica Recycle
2500 Michigan Ave., Santa Monica, CA 90404
(213) 458-8526
Even if you don't live in Santa Monica, this group will send you information on how and what to compost in your backyard or on your apartment balcony or patio.

Mr. Rumples Recycles, by Barbara Anne Coltharpe
Hyacinth House: Baton Rouge, 1989. $5.25. Available at bookstores, or from:
Hyacinth House Publishers
P.O. Box 14603, Baton Rouge, LA 70898
A twenty-five-page book on recycling and composting for children grades kindergarten through sixth.

SUPPLIES

Compost starters can be found in many nurseries (especially those that sell compost bins). The Ringer starter is one that many experts recommend. You can also find thermometers to test the compost's temperature, but this isn't a necessity.

MAIL ORDER:

Gardener's Supply
128 Intervale Rd., Burlington, VT 05401
(802) 863-1700
Here find compost thermometers, Bio-Activators to help heat up your compost pile, garden sieves in two sizes to sift compost before you throw it on the garden, and many other supplies.

Gardens Alive!
Natural Gardening Research Center
Hwy. 48, Box 149, Sunman, IN 47041
(812) 623-3800
If you want to make compost faster, you'll want a starter like Compost Alive!

Peaceful Valley Farm Supply
P.O. Box 2209, Grass Valley, CA 95945
(916) 272-4769
In addition to offering a steel tube that aerates your compost pile, and a thermometer, this is one of the few sources we've seen for soil sifters to remove rocks and large pieces of material from compost.

Bargyla Rateaver, Ph.D.
9049 Covina St., San Diego, CA 92126
(619) 566-8994
Here's another source of a compost starter culture to speed up the transformation process, plus a source of answers to your composting questions.

Ringer
9959 Valley View Rd., Eden Prairie, MN 55344-3585
(800) 654-1047
Ringer can help you make compost in a large plastic bag, using Brown Leaf Compost Maker, Compost Plus, or Grass Clippings Compost Maker. These starters are formulated with microorganisms, enzymes, and nutrients to turn leaves, twigs, pine needles, and grass into rich humus.

Territorial Seed Company
P.O. Box 157, Cottage, OR 97424
942-9547

Territorial carries compost thermometers, aerators, and Bio-Activator.

CONCRETE, see RECYCLED PRODUCTS

*d*IAPERS ....

BIODEGRADABLE PAPER DIAPERS

Cotton diapers are always better for the environment than even the best biodegradable diapers, which are made from wood pulp. But if you need disposables occasionally, these are worth serious consideration. (To find them locally check our listings for stores that sell organic baby food.) Use them with diaper covers. And please, use them sparingly. Home washing and diaper services are the most ecologically sound ways to go.

MAIL ORDER:

Co-op America
c/o Order Service
10 Farrell St., South Burlington, VT 05403
(800) 456-1177

"Dovetails" are made of wood pulp with a soft rayon cover. They biodegrade in one month (given the right conditions); from $25 to $28 for about a hundred, plus shipping.

Seventh Generation
Colchester, VT 05446-1672
(800) 456-1177

The soft, leak-proof diapers made from BCTMP (bleached chemi-thermal mechanical pulp) are bleached with hydrogen peroxide rather than polluting chlorine. They leave no dioxin residue. For a package of forty-four to twenty-eight, depending on size, the price is $11.95 per package, or four packages for $44.50. Home-delivery service and monthly shipments are offered too.

Also available are diapers bleached with hydrogen peroxide that use half the wood pulp of other disposables with same absorbency. They come sixty to twenty-eight per package, depending on size; $12 per package or four packages for $44.50, plus shipping.

COTTON DIAPERS

You can find these at almost any department store (J.C. Penny's, Sears, Toys R Us). We've listed sources of some unusual, innovative designs.

WILLAMETTE VALLEY
Sundance Natural Foods
748 E. Twenty-fourth Ave., Eugene, OR 97401
343-9142
Sundance carries the one-piece diaper, Bumpkins.

Earth Mercantile
6344 S.W Capitol Hwy., Portland, OR 97201
246-4935
Contoured cotton diapers by Rainbow, Nikky cotton diaper covers, cotton terry wipes, and nursing pads.

If Not Now...When?
512 N.W. Twenty-first Ave., Portland, OR 97209
222-4471
If Not Now...When? has Bumpkins, a one-piece diaper with a waterproof nylon cover and thick cotton padding, and Bumpkins' 100 percent cotton, flushable diaper liners.

MANUFACTURERS:
Encourage your local stores to carry these innovative cotton diapers, and call for the store nearest you.
Baby Bunz & Co.
P.O. Box 1717, Sebastopol, CA 95473
(707) 829-5347
Baby Bunz offers Nikkys, a breathable diaper in cotton or wool felt.

Biobottoms
Box 6009, 3820 Bodega Ave., Petaluma, CA 94953
(707) 778-7945
The breathable wool diaper covers are Velcro fastened and can last five diaper changes before washing.

Bumpkins
(800) 553-9302

Cotton padding with waterproof nylon outer shell and Velcro fasteners; eliminates the need for plastic pants; $60 to $90 per dozen. Bumpkins also has disposable cotton liners.

Diaperaps
(800) 477-3424
Cotton padding with a thin foam plus nylon lining and Velcro fasteners; $64 to $90 per dozen. Call for the store nearest you.

DIAPER SERVICES

Exchanging used cotton diapers for clean ones is another alternative to disposable diapers; look in the Yellow Pages under Diaper Services. If you cannot easily find one, contact:
National Association of Diaper Services
2017 Walnut St., Philadelphia, PA 19103
(215) 569-3650

DRAPES, INSULATED, see INSULATION

DRIP IRRIGATION, see WATER

elected officials to lobby

If you're unhappy with a political environmental stand, write your public officials. If you support a candidate's position, consider a donation, or volunteer time to ensure that he or she is elected. The Oregon League of Conservation Voters (OLCV) rates and publishes the environmental records of most candidates and will gladly send you this information.

Oregon League of Conservation Voters
506 S.W. Sixth Ave., Ste. 1004, Portland, OR 97204
224-4011

POLITICIANS AT THE STATE LEVEL

Gov. Barbara Roberts
State Capitol Building, Salem, OR 97310
(800) 322-6345

Rep. Ron Cease and Sen. Dick Springer
Cochairs, Joint Interim Committee on Energy, Environment, and Hazardous Materials
State Capitol Building, Salem, OR 97310
378-8179

Your local state representative and senator
State Capitol Building, Salem, OR 97310
If you're not sure who represents you, get in touch with the State Elections Division, State Capitol Building, Salem, OR 97310, 378-4144. From Portland call 222-1963.

OREGON POLITICIANS AT THE NATIONAL LEVEL

Rep. Les AuCoin
2159 Rayburn House Office Bldg., Washington, DC 20515-3701
(202) 225-0855, (503) 326-2901

Rep. Peter Defazio
1233 Longworth House Office Bldg., Washington, DC 20515-3705
(202) 225-6416, (503) 465-6732

Rep. Mike Kopetski
1520 Longworth House Office Bldg., Washington, DC 20515-3705
(202) 225-5711, (503) 588-9100

Rep. Bob Smith
118 Cannon House Office Bldg., Washington, DC 20515-3702
(202) 225-6730, (503) 776-4646

Rep. Ron Wyden
2452 Rayburn House Office Bldg., Washington, DC 20515-3703
(202) 225-4811, (503) 231-2300

Sen. Mark O. Hatfield
SH-711 Hart Senate Office Bldg., Washington, DC 20510-3701
(202) 224-3753, (503) 326-3386

Sen. Bob Packwood
SR-259 Russell Senate Office Bldg., Washington, DC 20510-3702
(202) 224-5244, (503) 221-3370

*e*NERGY EXTENSION SERVICE, OREGON STATE UNIVERSITY

The Energy Extension Service offers educational programs, activities, information, and materials on a wide range of energy issues. We have found both the statewide-office and regional field staffs friendly and always willing to help.

STATEWIDE
Oregon State University
Batcheller Hall #344, Corvallis, OR 97331-2405
737-3004
Contact David Philbrick, energy program leader; Greg Wheeler, commercial/industrial energy specialist and director of the Energy Analysis & Diagnostic Center; or W. S. (Gus) Baker, commercial energy/lighting specialist.

NORTHWEST OREGON
Energy Extension Service
1530 S.W. Taylor St., Portland, OR 97204
241-9172
Contact David Brook or Ted Haskell, energy agents.

WEST CENTRAL OREGON
Energy Extension Service
950 W. Thirteenth St., Eugene, OR 97402
687-4243
Contact Bryan Boe, energy agent.

SOUTHWEST OREGON
Energy Extension Service
1301 Maple Grove Dr., Medford, OR 97501
776-7371
Contact Larry Giardina, energy agent.

CENTRAL OREGON
Energy Extension Service
1128 N.W. Harriman St., Bend, OR 97701
388-6436
Contact Tom Wykes, energy agent.

EASTERN OREGON
Energy Extension Service
Rt. 1, Box 1705, La Grande, OR 97850
963-1010
Contact David Kooer, energy agent.

*e*NVIRONMENTAL ACTION GROUPS

Good news; environmental groups are springing up all over Oregon. Concerned citizens see an abuse, organize, and take a stand. Since many of these are small grass-roots organizations without telephone numbers, we have not listed them all. But we did discover a group, Environmental Communications Network (ECN), with a computer data base listing more than ninety different environmental groups. If you call with your location and environmental concern, ECN can connect you with the right person.

ECN also offers a speakers' bureau, a communications training program, and an information and referral service. The group can tell you about environmental job opportunities, conferences, and newsletters and itself offers courses in conflict management and negotiation techniques applied to environmental issues.

Environmental Communications Network (ECN)
519 S.W. Park Ave. #205, Portland, OR 97205
228-6690
Contact Wendy Ice.

WILLAMETTE VALLEY
Santiam Wilderness Committee
7665 N.E. McDonald Circle, Corvallis, OR 97330
745-5496
Contact Pat Loveland.

Siuslaw Task Force
P.O. Box 863, Corvallis, OR 97339
754-6261
Contact Steve Kratka.

Friends of the Illinois River
477 Mary Ln., Eugene, OR 97405

484-4820
Contact David Atkin.

Friends of the Three Sisters
336 Ventura Ave., Eugene, OR 97405
344-9848
Contact Lois Schreiner.

Land Air and Water (LAW)
University of Oregon Law School, Eugene, OR 97403
346-3828
Contact Penelope Buell.

The Native Forest Council
P.O. Box 2171, Eugene, OR 97402
688-2600
Brings public attention to the destruction of national forests through petitions, the media, and legislation.

Northwest Coalition for Alternatives to Pesticides (NCAP)
P.O. Box 1393, Eugene, OR 97204
344-5044
Educates people about the hazards of pesticides and the availability of alternatives.

Oregon Rivers Council
P.O. Box 309, Eugene, OR 97440
345-0119
Concerned with river pollution and the destruction of watersheds.

Save Our ecoSystem, Inc. (SOS)
407 W. Blair St., Eugene, OR 97402
484-2679
Works with BLM officials to hold off pesticide spraying. SOS is also a source of recycled and unbleached products and other ecology items.

Southern Willamette Green Assembly
1117 W. Eleventh Ave., Eugene, OR 97401
Green hotlines 344-5296, 344-5521
Based on the international Green movement, the local group promotes ecological wisdom, economic justice, and postpatriarchal values. Projects

in Eugene include the Green House, a model "eco-home," and community education.

Survival Center
Erb Memorial Union, Ste. 1, University of Oregon, Eugene, OR 97403
686-4356
Finds creative solutions for the environmental threats of our day. Projects include ancient-forest hikes; the Opal Creek Defense Coalition, Rainforest Action group, and Youth Greens; offshore drilling, dolphins and driftnets, recycling and precycling, animal rights.

McKenzie Guardians
51013 McKenzie Hwy., Finn Rock, OR 97488
822-3379
Contact Jim Baker or Judith Baker.

Sierra Club
2121 Fourteenth Ave., Forest Grove, OR 97116
357-6818
The club's 7,200 Oregon members are concerned with all aspects of the environment. It has chapters in La Grande-Pendleton, Portland, Bend, Klamath Falls, Eugene, Corvallis, Salem, Medford, and Lincoln City.

The Environmental Party
23005 N. Coburg Rd., Harrisburg, OR 97446
995-6164
Supports an environmentally sound high-tech-assisted future that assures greater health, wealth, and human rights. Contact William Conde.

Association of Northwest Steelheaders
P.O. Box 2187, Lake Oswego, OR 97035
630-4582
Works for the preservation of native steelhead, trout, and salmon populations, with chapters around the state.

Friends of Bunker Hill
39450 Mohawk Loop, Marcola, OR 97454
933-2415
Contact Harold E. Hushbeck.

Audubon Society
5151 N.W. Cornell Rd., Portland, OR 97210
292-6855
Dedicated to the enjoyment, understanding, and protection of birds and other wildlife and their habitats. It has chapters in Corvallis, Eugene, Salem, Klamath Falls, Medford, Wolf Creek, Roseburg, Bend, Hood River, North Bend, and Port Orford.

Citizens Utility Board of Oregon (CUB)
921 S.W. Morrison St., Rm. 550, Portland, OR 97240
227-1984
Created by Oregon's voters in 1984, CUB works for responsible utility practices and policies. Its current focus is to establish public power in Portland.

Columbia-Willamette Greens
P.O. Box 8136, Portland, OR 97208
284-8870
A global grass-roots movement, the Greens work toward an environmental society with a sustainable future. At least fourteen autonomous "circles" exist in the Portland-Vancouver area. Open-circle events and workshops are held to further acquaint people with Greens ideas.

Conservation International
10 S.W. Ash St., Portland, OR 97201
227-6225
Focuses on the critically threatened tropical ecosystems. Through education and conservation training the group helps local decision makers set priorities.

Friends of Mount Hood
2637 S.W. Water St., Portland, OR 97201
223-9028

Friends of Trees
P.O. Box 40851, Portland, OR 97240
282-2155
Devoted to urban forestry, the Friends educate about the importance of trees globally, improve the environment by planting and caring for trees, and advocate policies that protect city trees.

Greenpeace Action
1437 S.W. Columbia St., Portland, OR 97210
241-1507
The world's largest environmental group is especially concerned with ocean ecology and wildlife, disarmament, and toxic waste including acid rain.

Izaac Walton League of America
1825 N.E. Ninety-second Ave., Portland, OR 97220
255-2070
Concerned with the wise stewardship of the land and its resources. There also are chapters in Eugene, Forest Grove, Mary's Peak, Nehalem Valley, Salem, Umpqua, and Union County.

Monarch Project of the Xerces Society
The Xerces Society
10 S.W. Ash St., Portland, OR 97204
222-2788
Preserves the overwintering sites of the monarch butterfly.

The Nature Conservancy
1205 N.W. Twenty-fifth Ave., Portland, OR 97210
228-9561
Committed to the global preservation of natural diversity. The conservancy finds, protects, and maintains the best examples of communities, ecosystems, and endangered species in the natural world.

Northwest Environmental Advocates
406 S.W. Second Ave., Portland, OR 97204
295-0490
Works for the protection of people and land from toxic wastes, water and air pollution, and nuclear facilities and radioactive wastes, through education, research, and legal advocacy.

1000 Friends of Oregon
534 S.W. Third Ave., Ste. 300, Portland, OR 97204
223-4396
Works for the protection of farm and forest lands from urban sprawl through public education, legal representation, and research.

Oregon Environmental Council
2637 S.W. Water Ave., Portland, OR 97201
222-1963
Advocates air and water purity, reduced exposure to hazardous materials and pesticides, sound mining and forest practices, recycling, land use, and energy planning. It has a chapter in Jacksonville.

Oregon League of Conservation Voters
506 S.W. Sixth Ave., Ste. 1004, Portland, OR 97204
224-4011
Dedicated to electing candidates who support conservation programs. A nonpartisan committee, OLCV holds our elected officials accountable by publishing voting records and also ratings based on these officials' votes on environmental legislation.

Oregon Natural Resources Council
522 S.W. Fifth Ave., Ste. 1050, Portland, OR 97204
223-9001
Works for the protection of Oregon's remaining ancient forests, rivers, oceans, coastline, and high desert wilderness.

Oregon State Public Interest Research Group (OSPIRG)
1536 S.E. Eleventh Ave., Portland, OR 97214
231-4181
Priorities include recycling and reducing the use of excess packaging and toxic chemicals. OSPIRG conducts independent research and monitors government and corporate actions. It also has offices at the University of Oregon (Eugene), Southern Oregon State College (Ashland), and during legislative sessions the state capital (Salem).

Oregon Trout
7830 S.W. Fortieth Ave., Portland, OR 97219
244-2292
Protects, restores, and promotes the natural productivity of Oregon's fish habitats and fish, especially wild trout, native steelhead, and salmon.

Recycling Advocates
2420 S.W. Boundary St., Portland, OR 97201
244-0026

Wants to maximize waste reduction and recycling. Projects include canvassing neighborhoods for curbside collection, implementing a plastic-can boycott and polystyrene foam ban, offering office paper recycling demonstrations, lobbying for better recycling systems, and a weekly *Oregonian* column entitled "Reduce, Reuse, Recycle."

River Network
3423 S.E. Hawthorne St., Portland, OR 97207
230-0488
Provides technical assistance, information, and various river saving tools to local river protection organizations.

WaterWatch
921 S.W. Morrison St., Ste. 534, Portland, OR 97205
295-4039
Promotes good environmental water policies for Oregon.

The Wilderness Society
610 S.W. Alder St., Portland, OR 97205
248-0452
Works for the preservation of wilderness areas and wildlife, and to build awareness of the relationship between man and his natural environment.

The Xerces Society
10 S.W. Ash St., Portland, OR 97204
222-2788
Protects the lower vertebrates.

Friends of Breitenbush Cascade
P.O. Box 482, Salem, OR 97308
585-8551
Contact Mark Ottanad.

Native Plant Society of Oregon
1920 Engel Ave. N.W., Salem, OR 97304
585-9419
Promotes knowledge and identification of Pacific Northwest native plants and protects Oregon's rare, threatened, and endangered plant species.

Oregon League of Women Voters
2659 Commercial St. S.E., Ste. 220, Salem, OR 97302
581-5722

The Oregon League of Women Voters is now concentrating on legislation that concerns offshore drilling and mining. Look in your phone book or call them at the number above to find the local chapter nearest you.

The Wetlands Conservancy
P.O. Box 1195, Tualatin, OR 97062
691-1394

Acquires wetlands through purchase or donation, to protect them. Jack Broome, president of this nonprofit land trust, will help anyone in the state interested in setting up a land trust.

SOUTHERN OREGON

Friends of the Greensprings
15096 Hwy. 66, Ashland, OR 97520
482-2307

Headwaters
P.O. Box 729, Ashland, OR 97520
482-4459

An educational group that protects watersheds in Southwest Oregon; Headwaters promotes public forest management, through citizen participation and legal challenges when necessary.

SALUD
P.O. Box 877, Phoenix, OR 97535
535-7164

Helps farm workers with pesticide problems.

Umpqua Wilderness Defenders
1262 Kester Rd., Roseburg, OR 97470
673-8697

Contact Michael Lund or Sheila Lund.

EASTERN AND CENTRAL OREGON

Blue Mountain Environmental Council
Rt. 1, Box 73, Baker City, OR 97814
523-7076

Concerned with the burning of hazardous wastes in Baker County and Federal forest issues. Contact Clark Miller.

Hells Canyon Preservation Council (HCPC)
P.O. Box 605, Joseph, OR 97846
476-4498

The Wallowa Resource Council
P.O. Box 843, Joseph, OR 97856
886-3501
Promotes the wise use of land in Wallowa County. The council has been involved in mining and logging issues, wilderness policy, recycling, and environmental education in the schools. Contact Janet Hohmann.

Blue Mountains Protection All
1108 Adams Ave., La Grande, OR 97850
936-3266
Contact Loren Hughes.

Grande Ronde Resources Council
96 Oak St., La Grande, OR 97850
963-7893
Contact Mike Daugherty or Sue Daugherty.

Lawnchairs for Peace
269 E. Hickory Union St., La Grande, OR 97850
562-6227
Concerned with the transport of nuclear waste from Hanford. Contact Jack Gruszczynski.

THE COAST
Woodworkers Alliance for Rainforest Protection (WARP)
P.O. Box 133, Coos Bay, OR 97420-0013
269-6907
Formed of woodworkers concerned with wood harvesting and tropical rain forest issues. The alliance holds conferences promoting sustainable forest management.

Gamebirds Unlimited
706 S.W. Hubert St., Newport, OR 97365
265-9854

This group is involved in the preservation of wildlife habitat and especially the wetlands of Lincoln County. It raises and releases blue grouse and mountain quail.

Friends of Elk River
P.O. Box 891, Port Orford, OR 97465
334-2555
Contact Jim Rogers.

Friends of the Oregon Coast
95295 Hwy. 101, Yachats, OR 97498
547-3424
Contact Tom Smith or Billiejo Smith.

*e*NVIRONMENTAL EDUCATION TOOLS AND SOURCES

John Inskeep Environmental Learning Center (ELC)
Clackamas Community College
19600 S. Molalla Ave., Oregon City, OR 97045
657-6958 x351

The John Inskeep ELC conducts nearly a hundred college classes in resource conservation, plants, and animals. A hundred thousand people visit it each year. Weather permitting, just as darkness falls you can view Mars, Saturn, and distant galaxies at the Haggart Memorial Astronomical Observatory. Make sure you come early and explore the full mile of wetlands and trails, over streams and around lakes, where you can observe the Wildlife Habitat Exhibit. Try to imagine that this was once an abandoned industrial site.

At the Alternative Technology Demonstration Site you will find fish rearing, solar exhibits (including a greenhouse), a wildflower testing area, a recycling center and conservation institute, urban streams, alternative waste systems, and a forty-minute demonstration with Northwest birds of prey.

Envirotrekking Tours: ELC offers twenty-two unique tours (some of them for Portland State University credit). The tours last from one to three days (transportation and lodging included) and cost between $40 and $430. Most are in the $100 range. With biologists, a geologist, and historians as guides, explore Mount St. Helens, ride rapids through the John Day River, follow the path of pioneers across the Oregon Trail, or trek with llamas through the Mount Jefferson Wilderness Area.

ENVIRONMENTAL EDUCATION

Hawk, the Environmental Storyteller: Through ELC, Hawk's storytelling is available to school groups or social organizations. Using song, dance, and stories from an authentic Native American powwow ceremony, he explains the precious relationship between animals, earth, and man.

Earth Mercantile
6344 S.W. Capitol Hwy., Portland, OR 97201
246-4935
Earth Mercantile is one of the new environmental stores, and it has fascinating products for every age group. Your children will enjoy, besides the book and game selections, puppets that change from a polliwog to a frog or from a caterpillar to a butterfly. It even has dinosaur mobiles and such nature-study toys as magnifying glasses. For the environmentally conscious adult the store has everything from safe deodorants to organic herb-growing kits and environmental starter kits.

Ecology House
341 S.W. Morrison St., Portland, OR 97204
223-4883
Besides books and nature paraphernalia Ecology House has a variety of environmental board games, like Endangered Species and Pollution Solution.

If Not Now...When?
512 N.W. Twenty-first Ave., Portland, OR 97209
222-4471
If Not Now...When? carries books and such children's games as A Beautiful Place and Oil Spill. It's an environmental store, carrying products that include recycled paper supplies, covers for your electrical outlets that block heat loss, and an electric moped.

The Nature Company
700 S.W. Fifth Ave., Portland, OR 97204
222-0015
Besides a wonderful book selection, The Nature Company has everything in nature paraphernalia from hickory walking sticks to telescopes.

NEED
7629 S.W. Hood St., Portland, OR 97201
244-1625

NEED develops student awareness of environmental issues in the school and community. It gives awards for environmental projects, sells participation kits ($17.50) to schools and clubs, and offers leadership training workshops for teachers.

EXTERMINATORS, *see* **PEST CONTROL**

FARMERS' MARKETS, *see* **FOOD**

FLOOR MATS, *see* **RECYCLED PRODUCTS**

*f*OOD, ORGANIC

BABY FOOD

The most popular brands of organic baby food found locally are Earth's Best and Simply Pure. A new baby food, In the Beginning, has just started production in Sweet Home, Oregon. Ask your supermarket to carry them if it doesn't already.

STATEWIDE
Fred Meyer, Inc.
Carries In the Beginning brand.

Ross IGA
Carries In the Beginning brand.

Safeway
Carries In the Beginning brand.

WILLAMETTE VALLEY
First Alternative
1007 S.E. Third St., Corvallis, OR 97333
753-3115
Carries Earth's Best.

Sunshine General Store
824 W. Main St., Cottage Grove, OR 97424
942-8836
Carries Earth's Best and Health Valley.

Friendly Foods and Deli
2757 Friendly St., Eugene, OR 97405
683-2079
Carries Earth's Best and Perlinger Naturals.

Kiva
125 W. Eleventh Ave., Eugene, OR 97401
342-8666
Carries Earth's Best.

New Frontier Market
Eighth Ave. & Van Buren St., Eugene, OR 97502
345-7401
Carries Earth's Best.

Oasis
2489 Willamette St., Eugene, OR 97405
345-1014
Carries In The Beginning, Pure & Simple, and Earth's Best.

Red Barn Grocery
357-A Van Buren St., Eugene, OR 97402
342-7503
Carries Earth's Best and Health Valley lines.

Sundance
748 E. Twenty-fourth Ave., Eugene, OR 97401
345-0141
Carries Earth's Best.

Daily Grind
4026 S.E. Hawthorne Blvd., Portland, OR 97214
223-5521
Carries Earth's Best.

Food Front Co-op Grocery
2375 N.W. Thurman St., Portland, OR 97210
222-5658
Carries Earth's Best.

Happy Harvest Grocery
2348 S.E. Ankeny St., Portland, OR 97214
235-5358
Carries Earth's Best.

Nature's Fresh Northwest
5909 S.W. Corbett St., Portland, OR 97219
244-3934
All four stores carry Earth's Best.

3449 N.E. Twenty-fourth Ave., Portland, OR 97212
288-3414

4000 S.W. 117th Ave., Beaverton, OR 97005
646-3824

6344 S.W. Capitol Hwy., Portland, OR 97225
144-3110

People's Food Store
3029 S.E. Twenty-first Ave., Portland, OR 97214
232-9051
Carries Earth's Best.

Heliotrope Natural Foods
2060 Market St. N.E., Salem, OR 97301
362-5487
Carries Earth's Best.

Perrywinkle Provisions
1101 Main St., Sweet Home, OR 97386
367-6614
Carries In The Beginning.

SOUTHERN OREGON
Ashland Community Food Store
37 Third St., Ashland, OR 97520
482-2237
Carries Earth's Best.

New Life Natural Foods
202 W. Lister St., Cave Junction, OR 97523

592-3816
Carries Earth's Best.

Harmony Natural Store
116 Main St., Rogue River, OR 97537
582-3075
Carries Earth's Best.

EASTERN AND CENTRAL OREGON

Nature's General Store
Wagner Mall, Bend, OR 97702
382-6732
Carries Earth's Best.

Wy' East
110 Eighth St., Hood River, OR 97031
386-8766
Carries Earth's Best.

Nature's Pantry Natural Food Store
1907 Fourth Ave., La Grande, OR 97850
963-7955
Carries Earth's Best.

Oregon Natural Market
340 S.W. Fifth St., Ontario, OR 97914
889-8714
Carries Foods for Health brand.

Cornucopia General Store
Wagner Square, Redmond, OR 97756
523-6281
Carries Earth's Best.

THE COAST

The Community Store, Inc.
1389 Duane St., Astoria, OR 97103
325-0027
Can special-order organic baby food.

Osburn's Grocery & Deli
240 N. Hemlock St., Cannon Beach, OR 97110
436-2234
Carries Earth's Best.

Trillium Natural Grocery
1026 S.E. Jetty Ave., Lincoln City, OR 97367
994-5665
Carries Earth's Best.

Oceana Co-op Natural Foods
415 N.W. Coast St., Newport, OR 97365
265-8285
Carries Earth's Best and Health Valley.

Grady's Market
580 N.E. Broadway, Waldport, OR 97394
563-3542
Carries Earth's Best.

MAIL ORDER:
Co-op America
c/o Order Service
10 Farrell St., South Burlington, VT 05403
(800) 456-1177

Simply Pure strained and diced fruits and vegetables come in cases of twelve or twenty-four. Nonmembers pay an extra $3.50 service charge per order; annual membership, $15 per year.

Seventh Generation
Colchester, VT 05446-1672
(800) 456-1177

This catalog house sells Earth's Best baby food by the case (twenty-four jars) or sampler pack (six jars), and also six-ounce canisters of organic instant cereals in three flavors.

Walnut Acres
Penns Creek, PA 17862
(800) 433-3998

One hundred percent certified organic fruits, vegetables, and cereals are made in Vermont and can be shipped to you monthly or by individual order. They are sold in 4.5-ounce jars, twenty-four jars to a case; sample packs are available, for a fee, of course.

FARMERS' MARKETS

At the Farmers' Markets sponsored by these groups you will find pesticide-free fruits, vegetables, sprouts, dried fruits, nuts, and natural honey. Some are certified organic; all food is fresh. You can speak directly with the growers. Some markets even have flowers, plants, and baked goods. If you want to know locations, times, and what produce is available, call the contact person at the phone number we provide.

WILLAMETTE VALLEY
Beaverton Farmers' Market
P.O. Box 4, Beaverton, OR 97005
643-5345
Contact Laurie McEachem.

Corvallis/Albany Area Mid-Willamette Growers Assoc.
26675 Starr Rd., Monroe, OR 97456
847-5641
Contact Jack Lawrence.

Gresham Farmers' Market
P.O. Box 422, Gresham, OR 97030
661-3777
Contact Lisa Barten-Mullins.

Hillsboro Farmers' Market
1618 Douglas St., Forest Grove, OR 97116
357-3518
Contact Merrill Lunlam.

Lane County Farmers' Market
P.O. Box 1714, Eugene, OR 97440
952-1577
Contact David Amorose.

McMinnville Farmers' Market
West Valley Farmers
12741 N. Hwy. 99 W., McMinnville, OR 97128
472-6154
Contact Sue Reschly.

Salem Public Market
11954 River Rd. N.E., Ervais, OR 97026
Contact Rose Machalek.

SOUTHERN OREGON
Grants Pass Farmers' Market
P.O. Box 573, Grants Pass, OR 97526
476-5375
Contact Marty Fate.

Medford Growers Market
P.O. Box 4041, Medford, OR 97501
855-1326
Contact Joyce Schillen.

Phoenix Farmers' Market
4880 S. Pacific Hwy., Phoenix, OR 97535
535-3234
Contact "Kim."

EASTERN AND CENTRAL OREGON
Blue Mountain Producers' Co-op
1207 M Ave., La Grande, OR 97440
963-8049
Contact Jenny Nicholson.

Harvest Sun Farmers' Market
P.O. Box 290, Sixes, OR 97476
Mobile phone 267-9038
Contact Melvin Sutton or Floyd Williams.

THE COAST
Lincoln County Small Growers Assoc.
9170 Alsea Hwy., Tidewater, OR 97390

528-3050
Contact June Reynolds.

PRODUCE

We look forward to the time when we can go to any supermarket and find produce labeled organic or nutriclean (pesticide free). This will happen if you ask the manager of your local market to order more. (Don't forget that when you also buy transitional organic produce you encourage more farmers to become organic.)

For the convenience of your local market manager we've listed distributors that any market can contact. Meanwhile the following stores carry some organic produce, and many also stock frozen organic foods as well.

You can trust any organic products certified by Oregon Tilth. Such products have passed laboratory tests on leaf tissue, water, and soil. The Tilth program also supports organic farmers, has a newsletter, publishes books, and puts on a Tilth Festival. For information about these contact the organization directly:

Oregon Tilth
P.O. Box 218, Tualatin, OR 97062
692-4877

Much of our organic food information came from the directory listed below. It also lists organic farmers and their crops, restaurants, organic food processors, and much more. For free copies send a legal-size self-addressed stamped envelope with $.45 postage for each directory requested. It's to be updated each year.

Organically Grown In Oregon
2016 S.E. Sherrett St., Portland, OR 97202
235-5034

STATEWIDE

Cub Foods
Food Connection
Fred Meyer, Inc.

WILLAMETTE VALLEY

Anzen Importers
4021 S.W. 117th Ave., Beaverton, OR 97005
627-0913

First Alternative
1007 S.E. Third Ave., Corvallis, OR 97333
753-3115

Sunshine General Store
824 W. Main St., Cottage Grove, OR 97424
942-8836

Down to Earth Home Store
Fifth Ave. & Olive St., Eugene, OR 97402
344-6357

Food Value
2102 Bailey Hill Rd., Eugene, OR 97405
686-1821
Carries organic produce at all four stores.

1960 Franklin Blvd., Eugene, OR 97503
343-6418

2750 River Rd., Eugene, OR 97404
688-0555

2858 Willamette St., Eugene, OR 97405
342-5779

Frederick's Food Warehouse
2025 River Rd., Eugene, OR 97404
688-1467

Friendly Foods and Deli
2757 Friendly St., Eugene, OR 97405
683-2079

Grower's Market
454 Willamette St., Eugene, OR 97405
687-1145

Kiva
125 W. Eleventh Ave., Eugene, OR 97401
342-8666

New Frontier Market
Eighth Ave. & Van Buren St., Eugene, OR 97502
345-7401

Oasis
2489 Willamette St., Eugene, OR 97405
345-1014
Oasis offers, besides organic produce, chemical-free meat from animals specially raised without growth stimulants, hormones, or steroids. Only necessary veterinary treatment is allowed. (Oregon Home Grown Meats, also in Eugene, has chemical-free meat too.)

Paradise Market & Deli
2390 Agate St., Eugene, OR 97403
345-4431

Red Barn Grocery
357-A Van Buren St., Eugene, OR 97402
342-7503

Sundance
748 E. Twenty-fourth Ave., Eugene, OR 97401
345-0141

Harvest Fresh Produce
1637 N. Baker St., McMinnville, OR 97128
472-5740

Bale's Thriftway
12675 N.W. Cornell Rd., Portland, OR 97006
627-0162

Busy Corner Grocery
4927 S.E. Forty-first Ave., Portland, OR 97202
774-0911

Cub Foods
1222 N.E. 102nd Ave., Portland, OR 97220
252-3353

Cub Foods Clackamas
11250 S.E. Eighty-second Ave., Portland, OR 97266
654-3210

Daily Grind
4026 S.E. Hawthorne Blvd., Portland, OR 97214
223-5521

Earth Mercantile
6344 S.W. Capitol Hwy., Portland, OR 97201
246-4935

Ecology House
341 S.W. Morrison St., Portland, OR 97204
223-4883

Food Front Co-op Grocery
2375 N.W. Thurman St., Portland, OR 97210
222-5658

Happy Harvest Grocery
2348 S.E. Ankeny St., Portland, OR 97214
235-5358

If Not Now...When?
512 N.W. Twenty-first Ave., Portland, OR 97209
222-4471

Kruger's Specialty Produce
1200 N.E. Broadway St., Portland, OR 97212
288-4236

Nature's Fresh Northwest
5909 S.W. Corbett St., Portland, OR 97219
244-3934
Carries organic produce at all four stores.

6344 S.W. Capitol Hwy., Portland, OR 97225
244-3110

3449 N.E. Twenty-fourth Ave., Portland, OR 97212
288-3414

4000 S.W. 117th Ave., Beaverton, OR 97005
646-3824

Pastaworks
3735 S.E. Hawthorne Blvd., Portland, OR 97214
232-1010

People's Food Store
3029 S.E. Twenty-first Ave., Portland, OR 97214
232-9051

Sheridan Produce
409 S.E. Martin Luther King Blvd., Portland, OR 97204
235-9353

Strohecker's Inc.
2855 S.W. Patton Rd., Portland, OR 97201
223-7391

Heliotrope Natural Foods
2060 Market St. N.E., Salem, OR 97301
362-5487
Ask to get on the store's mailing list for the free environmental newspaper *The Heliogram*.

Perrywinkle Provisions
1101 Main St., Sweet Home, OR 97386
367-6614

SOUTHERN OREGON
Ashland Community Food Store
37 Third St., Ashland, OR 97520
482-2237

Promise Natural Food Store
503 S. Main St., Canyonville, OR 97417
839-4167

Hammer's Model Market
202 S. Redwood Hwy., Cave Junction, OR 97523
592-3236

New Life Natural Foods
202 W. Lister St., Cave Junction, OR 97523
592-3816

The Herb Shop
145 S.E. G St., Grants Pass, OR 97526
479-3602
Carries organic herbs and will special-order organic produce for customers.

Harmony Natural Store
116 Main St., Rogue River, OR 97537
582-3075

Dee's Market
4601 Carnes Rd., Roseburg, OR 97470
679-7771
Carries organic produce at all four stores.

930 W. Harvard Blvd., Roseburg, OR 97470
673-8060

811 E. Central St., Sutherlin, OR 97479
459-2697

Hwy. 42, Winston, OR 97496
679-4028

New Day Quality Groceries
210 S.E. Jackson St., Roseburg, OR 97470
672-0275

Sutherlin Natural Foods
109 E. Central St., Sutherlin, OR 97479
459-3400

EASTERN AND CENTRAL OREGON
Greater Baker Food Co-op
2816 Tenth Ave., Baker, OR 97814
523-6281

Good Food Store
1124 N.W. Newport Ave., Bend, OR 97702
389-6533

Nature's General Store
Wagner Mall, Bend, OR 97702
382-6732

River Bend Country Store
2363 Tucker Rd., Hood River, OR 97031
386-8766

Wy' East
110 Eighth St., Hood River, OR 97031
386-6181

Nature's Pantry Natural Food Store
1907 Fourth Ave., La Grande, OR 97850
963-7955

Oregon Natural Market
340 S.W. Fifth St., Ontario, OR 97914
889-8714

Cornucopia General Store
Wagner Square, Redmond, OR 97756
523-6281

Apple Jack's
110 S. Spruce St., Sisters, OR 97759
549-5781

THE COAST
The Community Store, Inc.
1389 Duane St., Astoria, OR 97103
325-0027

Generous Helpings
604 Spruce St., Brookings, OR 97415
469-5414

Osburn's Grocery & Deli
240 N. Hemlock St., Cannon Beach, OR 97110
436-2234

Nosler's Natural Grocery
99 E. First St., Coquille, OR 97423
396-4823

Food Town Market
1665 Hwy. 101, Florence, OR 97439
997-2444

Bay Street General Store
1255 Bay St., Florence, OR 97439
997-7432

John's Fresh Produce
16044 Hwy. 101 S., Harbor, OR 97415
469-6421

Trillium Natural Grocery
1026 S.E. Jetty Ave., Lincoln City, OR 97367
994-5665

Oceana Co-op Natural Foods
415 N.W. Coast St., Newport, OR 97365
265-8285

Coos Head Food Store
1960 Sherman Ave., North Bend, OR 97459
756-7264

Grady's Market
580 N.E. Broadway St., Waldport, OR 97394
563-3542

DISTRIBUTORS:

Besides several distributors in the Willamette Valley and in Southern Oregon we've listed some in California and Washington that may service the markets in your town.

WILLAMETTE VALLEY

Organically Grown Co-op
2545-I Prairie Rd., Eugene, OR 97402
689-5320

United Grocers
6433 S.E. Lake Rd., Milwaukie, OR 97222
653-6330

Pacific Coast Fruit Company
201 N.E. Second Ave., Portland, OR 97232
234-6411

Pioneer Fruit Distributors
231 S.E. Alder St., Portland, OR 97214
234-1167

Honey Heaven Distributors
1225 Fairview Dr., Springfield, OR 97477
488-2747

SOUTHERN OREGON

Maranatha Distributing
710 Jefferson St., Ashland, OR 97520
488-2747

Fresh Express
706 S. Central St., Medford, OR 97504
773-4431

Melvin Sutton & Floyd Williams
P.O. Box 290, Sixes, OR 97476
Mobile phone 267-9038

CALIFORNIA

Wholefood Express
3134 Jacobs Ave., Eureka, CA 95501
(707) 445-3185

Mountain Peoples' Wholesale
110 Springhill Dr., Grass Valley, CA 95945
(916) 273-9531

WASHINGTON
Northwest Dietetic Supply
7036 S. 190th St., Kent, WA 98032
(206) 251-5220

Nutrasource
4005 Sixth Ave. S., Seattle, WA 98108
(206) 467-7190

FOUNDATION VENTS, see RECYCLED PRODUCTS

*G*ARDEN AND LAWN CARE, ORGANIC ....

Most landscapers and yard-care companies will provide organic services and solutions if you request them. We did find a few who prefer organic.

Cascadia Landscape Design
1661 Willamette St., Eugene, OR 97401
342-1160
This company can give you anything from an edible landscape to a Japanese garden. Contact Jude Hobbs.

Harmony Landscape & Design
1595 Mistletoe St., Eugene, OR 97402
484-6484
Besides consulting on garden design and providing organic lawn and garden care, Bruce and Barbara Allen even build arbors and trellises.

Native & Urban
90901 Coburg Rd., Eugene, OR 97401
344-4877
Holde Fink provides organic lawn care and yard work and is a consultant for emergent organic farmers.

Gregory Gardens
4131 S.W. Lee St., Portland, OR 97221
246-2714
Gregory not only designs landscapes but provides maintenance and construction.

Northern Groves
3328 S.E. Kelly St., Portland, OR 97202
232-1860
Northern Groves provides a gardening service, helps with design, and is a bamboo nursery.

Organic Lawn Care
P.O. Box 19513, Portland, OR 97219
224-5513
Services include aeration, organic fertilization, and nonchemical alternatives for fungus, disease, and weed control. The method is based on that of Organic Lawn Care in Minneapolis ([612] 331-8600) and is supported by the Sierra Club.

GLASS, see INSULATION

HAZARDOUS WASTE, see RECYCLING HAZARDOUS WASTE

INSECTICIDES, see PEST CONTROL

INSULATION

Before you take on any expensive insulation project, have a free energy audit: see under Weatherization. For more information on the kinds of insulation available and how to buy and install them, send $2 for the publication *Insulation* to:

American Council for an Energy-Efficient Economy
1001 Connecticut Ave. N.W. #535, Washington, DC 20036

CELLULOSE, see RECYCLED PRODUCTS

DRAPES AS INSULATION

Single-pane glass by itself is poor insulation. Even an ordinary white plastic or fabric window shade will help keep your home warm in winter and cool in summer, but there is a variety of specialty insulated products that do an even better job. You can find them at your local custom drapery store.

The best product we've found on the market is a pleated "solarized" shade with honeycomb micropleats lined with aluminum by Duette, made by Kirsch, that traps air like a storm window and gives added insulation to your rooms. It's more expensive than other shades but does the best job. It comes in two styles and can be customized to fit arched windows.

WILLAMETTE VALLEY

Benson's Floor Covering
630 S. Lion St., Albany, OR 97321
926-8846

Whitaker Paint
324 S. Main St., Albany, OR 97321
928-8824

Lewis Paints
214 S.W. Second St., Corvallis, OR 97333
757-8551

E.G. Gardner Co.
P.O. Box 11290, Eugene, OR 97440
485-6984

Imperial Floors
355 Lincoln St., Eugene, OR 97401
342-5031

Vasona Shade
749 Madison St., Eugene, OR 97402
484-0159

Nice Furniture and Appliance
P.O Box 329, McMinnville, OR 97128
472-7322

Bollinger Window Fashions and Interiors
1501 N.E. Broadway, Portland, OR 97322
281-1236

Hillsdale Draperies
6360 S.W. Capitol Hwy., Portland, OR 97201
244-7563

Kathy's Karpets and Interiors
8425 S.W. Terwilliger Blvd., Portland, OR 97219
246-1121

Grant's Draperies
1204 Thirty-fifth Ave. N.W., Salem, OR 97304
362-9619

SOUTHERN OREGON

Ashland Interiors
293 E. Main St., Ashland, OR 97520
482-5830

Draperies-N-Things
538 N.E. E St., Grants Pass, OR 97526
479-5519

Jim's Floor Covering Shop
301 S. Front St., Medford, OR 97501
773-8291

New Trend Decorating Center
33 S. Riverside St., Medford, OR 97501
773-6312

EASTERN AND CENTRAL OREGON

Macomber
615 N.W. Tenth Ave., Pendleton, OR 97801
276-5386

THE COAST

Wayne's Color Centre
1000 Bay Shore Dr., Coos Bay, OR 97420
267-2010

The Interior Corner
422 N. Roosevelt Dr., Seaside, OR 97138
738-9440

GLASS AS INSULATION

Standard single-pane glass is a poor insulator, but double- or triple-paned glass with air between (thermal panes) and low-emissivity glass (known as Low-E, in the trade) are two answers to your insulation problems. The coating that's used on Low-E glass can cut heat loss up to 66 percent, and it can be applied to one of the two panes of glass in any double-insulated thermal applications. Any glazier can find thermal-pane and Low-E glass for you.

WEATHERSTRIPPING

You can find weatherstripping in all hardware stores. There's a new product that never sticks or loses its shape and that provides better insulation from heat and cold, too. The do-it-yourselfer can install this system with a special router; you may decide to have it installed for you. It will last as long as your house without needing to be replaced. As yet there are no Oregon outlets for this product, but you can order it from:

Weatherbead Insulation Systems, Inc.
5321 Derry Ave. #F, Agoura Hills, CA 91301
(818) 597-8291

WINDOW FILMS AND TINTING

Solar window films are available from stores specializing in both window shades and glass. To find tinters check in the Yellow Pages under Window Tinting. All major towns in Oregon have it listed. If it's not in your phone book call Brian Platt, president of Oregon Window Tinters, and he'll direct you to the nearest tinting service.

The main benefit of tinting is heat reduction. Glass that's been tinted also filters ultraviolet light, is stronger, and reduces glare.

Valley Vinyl
820 S. Front St., Central Point, OR 97502
664-4773
Contact Brian Platt.

Paul Austin Window Tint
P.O. Box 13382, Salem, OR 97309
Portland 246-3611
Eugene 343-6565
Salem 588-8585

Paul Austin Window Tint is the only outlet in the state that deals exclusively with solar window films and window tinting. Prices vary from $2 to $10 per square foot. The company works all over the state, depending on job size. Its films will stop 75 percent of the solar heat load, and therefore can be an alternative to air conditioning. In the winter top-performance films minimize heat loss.

*I*NVESTMENTS, SOCIALLY RESPONSIBLE ....

CREDIT CARDS

American Rivers
801 Pennsylvania Ave. S.E., Washington, DC 20003
Main office (202) 547-6900
Credit card information (704) 488-2175

Co-op America
2100 M St. N.W., Ste. 310, Washington, DC 20036
(800) 424-2667

Defenders of Wildlife
1244 Nineteenth St. N.W., Washington, DC 20036
(800) 972-9979, (202) 659-9510

International Fund for Animal Welfare
411 Main St., Yarmouth Port, MA 02675
(800) 972-9979, (508) 362-4944

National Business Association Credit Union
3807 Otter St., Bristol, PA 19007
(800) 441-0878

National Wildlife Confederation
1400 Sixteenth St. N.W., Washington, DC 20036
(800) 847-7378, (202) 797-6800

The Nature Conservancy
1815 N. Lynn St., Arlington, VA 22209
(703) 841-5300

The Wilderness Society
1400 Eye St. N.W., Washington, DC 20005
(202) 842-3400

Working Assets Funding Service
230 California St., San Francisco, CA 94111-9876
(415) 989-3200 (collect)

FINANCIAL ADVISORS

The financial advisors listed here are members of the Social Investment Forum (SIF).

WILLAMETTE VALLEY

Laurie McClain
Progressive Securities
767 Willamette St., Ste. 301, Eugene, OR 97401
345-5669

Scott Pope
Progressive Securities
767 Willamette St., Ste. 301, Eugene, OR 97401
345-5669

Shirley Raven
Raven Investment Services
442 Charnelton St., Eugene, OR 97401
344-3580

Thomas H. Roehl
Holbrook, Roehl & Sittner
1050 Willagillespie Rd., Eugene, OR 97401
683-2085

Rob Baird
Progressive Securities
5200 S.W. Macadam Ave., Ste. 350, Portland, OR 97201
224-7828

Allen T. Denison
Black & Co.

One S.W. Columbia St., Portland, OR 97258
248-7567

Ed DeWald
Security Pacific Bank
1001 S.W. Sixth Ave., Portland, OR 97208
222-7513

Carsten Henningsen
Progressive Securities
5200 S.W. Macadam Ave., Ste. 350, Portland, OR 97201
224-7828

Troy W. Horton
First Affiliated Securities
10136 S.W. Washington St., Portland, OR 97225
(800) 248-1173

Robert Jaquiss
Discover
1001 S.W. Fifth Ave., Ste. 1000, Portland, OR 97204
223-2884

Glenna Klepper
Security Pacific Bank
Private Banking
1001 S.W. Fifth Ave., Ste. 1200, Portland, OR 97204
796-3801

Shelly MacFarland
Dain Bosworth
One S.W. Columbia St., Ste. 1400, Portland, OR 97258
241-7020

Jan Schorey
Progressive Securities
5200 S.W. Macadam Ave., Ste. 350, Portland, OR 97201
224-7828

Steve Silver
Dean Witter

10260 S.W. Greenburg Rd. #300, Portland, OR 97228
(800) 452-5690

Ron Kelemen
Interwest Financial Advisors, Inc.
1500 Liberty St. S.E., Ste. 100, Salem, OR 97302
581-6020

SOUTHERN OREGON
Linda Datz
Gardner, Monosoff, Rumer, Datz
1380 Oleander St., Ste. C, Medford, OR 97504
779-4088

Barbara A. Rumer
Gardner, Monosoff, Rumer, Datz
1380 Oleander St., Ste. C, Medford, OR 97504
779-4088

INFORMATION

The financial services firms listed here specialize in socially responsible investing and financial planning. When you want to know which investments are best, not only for the environment but for your particular retirement needs and tax bracket, their brokers can help you compile information with which to draw conclusions. Some of the companies provide additional information on corporations and their impact on the environment. By getting general information from brokers, reading the prospectuses carefully, and pursuing further data on corporations listed in the prospectuses, you can develop a full picture of where your investment dollars are going. (See also the Publications section on Socially Responsible Investments.)

Advest, Inc.
124 Mount Auburn St., Cambridge, MA 02138
(800) 876-6673
A financial services company.

Boettcher and Co.
828 Seventeenth St., Denver, CO 80202

(800) 525-6482
A financial services company.

Council on Economic Priorities
30 Irving Pl., New York, NY 10003
(212) 420-1133
A nonprofit research organization, CEP reviews corporate performances as they affect society.

Data Center
464 Nineteenth St., Oakland, CA 94612
(415) 835-4692
A nonprofit library, the Data Center follows seven thousand corporations and four hundred publications.

First Affirmative Financial Network
410 N. Twenty-first St. #203, Colorado Springs, CO 80904
(800) 422-7284
A full-service brokerage firm in partnership with Co-op America, the network offers a free financial review questionnaire.

LOCAL CAPITAL RESOURCES

Northwest Capital Network (NCN)
P.O. Box 6650, Portland, OR 97228-6650
294-0643
A nonprofit business/investor referral service, NCN brings together entrepreneurs who require capital with investors who seek specific venture opportunities.

1 Percent Well Spent!
Metropolitan Service District (Metro)
2000 S.W. First Ave., Portland, OR
221-1646
Since 1988 Metro has set aside 1 percent of the Solid Waste Department's budget to fund innovative recycling programs. Now, for 1990-1991, approximately $350,000 has been earmarked for small-scale pilot projects that might not otherwise find funding. Individuals, private businesses, public/private consortiums, public agencies, and nonprofit organizations are eligible.

Projects for any type of waste reduction or recycling are considered. For 1990-1991 the emphasis will be on marketing—either by developing new markets for recovered materials or creating new products or equipment for existing markets. Projects may be technical or educational.

Proposed projects should include some of the following characteristics:
- be small in scale, with the ability to grow;
- emphasize market developments;
- recycle a high volume of material;
- send a low volume of by-products to the landfill;
- emphasize reduction of waste at source, or "precycling";
- be cost effective and manageable;
- be economically feasible and self-sustaining;
- be publicly acceptable;
- be environmentally sound and nonpolluting;
- include innovative processing techniques;
- offer direct benefits to the tri-county region;
- provide incentives for more recycling;
- involve women and/or minorities.

For more information, contact Judith Mandt or Leigh Zimmerman in Metro's Solid Waste Department at 221-1646.

Oregon Resource and Technology Development Corporation (ORTDC)
1934 N.E. Broadway, Portland, OR 97232-1502
282-4462
Fax (503) 280-6080

A lottery-funded state agency charged with building businesses in Oregon, ORTDC provides seed capital for ventures that meet these requirements:
- have potential for profitable growth;
- offer projected returns sufficient to attract additional investment;
- add value to Oregon-based resources;
- are Oregon-based companies or enterprises serving markets outside of Oregon for which national or international competition exists;
- document appropriate product and marketing research and sufficient management skills.

LOCAL INVESTMENTS

ARABLE
P.O. Box 5230, Eugene, OR 97405
485-7630

Established in 1984, the Association for Regional Agriculture Building the Local Economy provides capital for intensive small-scale farming, particularly organic farming; provides technical assistance for growers; develops new markets; educates consumers; and lobbies local and state government for favorable agricultural policies.

Individuals and organizations may lend money to ARABLE; there is a $25 minimum. Up to 6 percent interest is paid quarterly. Membership is open to everyone, but no more than 25 percent of ARABLE's total assets may be from outside its geographic area—Linn, Benton, and Lane counties.

LONG-DISTANCE TELEPHONE PLANS

The Nature Conservancy/MCI
The Nature Conservancy
1815 N. Lynn St., Arlington, VA 22209
(703) 841-5300

Working Assets/Sprint Plus
230 California St., San Francisco, CA 94111-9876
(800) 669-8585

MONEY-MARKET FUNDS

The funds listed below are considered by many brokers to be among the most responsibly managed available. Read all prospectuses carefully before investing.

Calvert SIF: Money Market Funds
4550 Montgomery Ave., Ste. 1000, Bethesda, MD 20814
(800) 368-2748
Negative Screens: South Africa, Weapons, Nuclear power
Positive Screens: Environmental protection, Good employee relations, Minority advancement

Working Assets
230 California St., San Francisco, CA 94111

(800) 533-3863
Negative Screens: South Africa, Military contractors, Nuclear power
Positive Screens: Housing, Equal opportunity education, Small businesses, Energy efficiency

MUTUAL FUNDS

The funds listed below are considered by many brokers to be among the most responsibly managed available. Read all prospectuses carefully before investing.

Calvert-Ariel Appreciation Fund
4550 Montgomery Ave., Ste. 1000, Bethesda, MD 20814
(800) 368-2748
Objective is growth.
Negative Screens: South Africa, Weapons, Nuclear power
Positive Screens: Environmentally sound companies with secure markets and strong reputations

Calvert Social Investment Funds
4550 Montgomery Ave., Ste. 1000, Bethesda, MD 20814
(800) 368-2748
Negative Screens: South Africa, Weapons, Nuclear power
Positive Screens: Environmental protection, Good employee relations, Minority advancement, Product safety

Calvert SIF: a bond fund. Objective is income.
Calvert SIF: an equity fund. Objective is growth.
Calvert SIF: a managed growth fund. Objective is balanced income and growth.

Dreyfus Third Century
666 Old Country Rd., Garden City, NY 11530
(800) 645-6561
Objective is growth.
Negative Screens: South Africa
Positive Screens: Environmental protection, Occupational health and safety, Equal opportunity employment

New Alternatives
295 Northern Blvd., Great Neck, NY 11021
(516) 466-0808

Objective is investment in alternative energy sources.
Negative Screens: Nuclear power, South Africa, Weapons
Positive Screens: Alternative energy, Occupational health and safety, Resource recovery

Parnassus Fund
295 California St., San Francisco, CA 94111
(800) 999-3505
Objective is growth.
Negative Screens: Alcohol and tobacco, Weapons, Nuclear power, South Africa
Positive Screens: Out-of-favor companies, Quality products, Good employee relations, Community participation, Progressive and enlightened management

Pax World Fund
224 State St., Portsmouth, NH 03801
(800) 767-1729
Objective is balanced income and growth.
Negative Screens: Weapons, South Africa, Alcohol, Tobacco, Gambling, Nuclear power
Positive Screens: Life-support products and services, Equal opportunity, Pollution control

Schield Progressive Environmental Fund
390 Union Blvd., Denver, CO 80228
(800) 826-8154
Objective is growth.
Negative Screens: EPA violators and polluters
Positive Screens: Environmental protection, Environmental soundness, Alternative energy

SFT Environmental Awareness Fund
1016 W. Eighth Ave., King of Prussia, PA 19406
(800) 523-2044
Objective is growth.
Negative Screens: (None)
Positive Screens: Environmental protection, Alternative energy, Waste management

PROFESSIONAL GROUPS

Pacific Northwest Chapter of SIF
P.O. Box 69625, Portland, OR 97201
236-2980
A volunteer group of investors and financial advisors, it publishes a quarterly newsletter and sponsors conferences on responsible investing. Contact Dan Walters.

Social Investment Forum (SIF)
430 First Ave. N., Ste. 290, Minneapolis, MN 55401
(612) 333-8338
Fax (612)342-2212

LIGHT BULBS, COMPACT FLUORESCENT

While 90 percent of the energy in a regular incandescent light bulb produces heat, not light, a compact fluorescent bulb (CFB) uses phosphorus to concentrate a small amount of energy into a lot of light. You can test this. The energy in a CFB is so low you can touch it anytime without the fear of being burned.

CFBs not only save electricity (up to $40 over a bulb lifetime) but reduce air pollution, and they outlast store-bought bulbs tenfold. Two kinds are sold locally; one (PL) requires an adapter, the other (SL) does not. We'll see a wide variety of CFBs on the market shortly. Experts recommend using PLs in offices where the light remains on for long periods of time and SLs in the home.

Equivalence of Compact Fluorescent Bulbs and Incandescent Bulbs

COMPACT FLUORESCENT	INCANDESCENT
5 watts	25 watts
7 watts	40 watts
9 watts	60 watts
18 watts	75 watts
28 watts	100 watts

STATEWIDE

Ace Hardware
All stores carry both SL and PL bulbs.

Durotest
(800) 776-1191

You may order either wholesale or retail compact fluorescent light bulbs (XL-escents) in various sizes. No adapter necessary.

Fred Meyer, Inc.
At Freddy's you can choose from four different fluorescent bulbs that already have the adapter attached.

Pay 'N Pack

True Value Hardware
Carries 27-watt SL fluorescent bulbs.

WILLAMETTE VALLEY
Pacific Lamp
10725 S.W. Fifth Ave., Beaverton, OR 97005
643-6516
Pacific Lamp invites you to see its demonstration of exactly how much energy is used by a CFB compared with a regular bulb. This company sells wholesale or retail.

Builder's Square
1160 N. Hayden Meadows Dr., Portland, OR 97217
286-0074

2315 S.E. Eighty-second Ave., Portland, OR 97215
775-0040

Earth Mercantile
6345 S.W. Capitol Hwy., Portland, OR 97201
246-4935
Includes adapters, and sizes vary from small to floodlight.

Fox Lamp & Furniture Co.
923 S.E. Hawthorne Blvd., Portland, OR 97214
233-8035
Sells both wholesale and retail.

If Not Now...When?
512 N.W. Twenty-first Ave., Portland, OR 97209
222-4471
Carries both SL and PL.

People's
3029 S.E. Twenty-first Ave., Portland, OR 97202
232-9051
Carries the Staco brand CFB.

American Fluorescent
565 Twenty-first Ave. S.E., Salem, OR 97309
(800) 547-7831, (503) 585-9535

THE COAST
Classic Lighting and Designs
1080 N. Coast Hwy., Newport, OR 97365
265-5882

Perry Electric
3131 Broadway, North Bend, OR 97459
756-2051

MAIL ORDER:
EcoSource
9051 Mill Station Rd., Bldg. E, Sebastopol, CA 95472
(800) 688-8345
CFBs that are electronically ballasted to screw into standard light sockets come in 18-watt to 27-watt sizes for $25 to $29. Ten-watt CFB floodlights with a glare shield are from $41 to $55. DULUX "EL" compacts range from 7 watts to 20 watts, for $23.95 to $24.95. EcoSource also carries Ecoworks energy-efficient incandescent bulbs as a nuclear-free alternative to bulbs made by nuclear weapons manufacturers—GE, GTE Sylvania, and Phillips.

Real Goods
966 Mazzoni St., Ukiah, CA 95482
(800) 762-7325
Carries a wide variety of CFBs with adapters, including outdoor floodlights, globe bulbs, and quad tube bulbs, which are shorter than other varieties of CFBs. To keep from being confused about all the energy alternatives you may want to send for Real Goods' *Alternative Energy Sourcebook* ($10); it has thirty-eight pages just on energy-efficient lighting.

Solar Electric
116 Fourth St., Santa Rosa, CA 95401

(800) 832-1986, (707) 542-1900
Fax (707) 542-4358

The DULUX "EL" lamp in 11-watt and 15- watt sizes are $24 and $25. With a built-in high-frequency electronic ballast they screw into standard 120-watt AC light fixtures. Also, in the 15-watt size, a round "globe" bulb (4 by 6 1/2 inches) or a "tube" bulb (3 by 6 3/4 inches) is one for $16.95 and five for $78.50.

LIGHT-RAIL TRANSIT, see PUBLIC TRANSPORTATION

LOGS, see RECYCLED PRODUCTS

LOW-E GLASS, see INSULATION

MANURE, see SOIL AMENDMENTS, ORGANIC

MASS TRANSIT, see PUBLIC TRANSPORTATION

NATIVE OREGON PLANTS

The usual rationalization for native plants is that they are disease free, low maintenance, and beautiful, and they attract wildlife. Overall this may be true, but for no other reason than their uniqueness to the Northwest, they deserve our attention.

INFORMATION SOURCES AND PLANT SOCIETIES

Hortus Northwest
P.O. Box 955, Canby, OR 97013
266-7968

The directory *Hortus Northwest* is published by Dale Shank. It not only lists 617 species of native Northwest plants but tells where you can obtain them, how to use them, and other information about the plants.

Aesthetic Floramania
36751 S. Hibbard Rd., Molalla, OR 97038
829-7236

Kate Gruitter stresses the importance of planting in the right place and is willing to answer your questions about native plants. (She sells only wholesale.)

Cascadia Native Landscape Center
P.O. Box 82292, Portland, OR 97282
236-0395
The center sponsors an annual conference on using native plants, and supplies native plant landscaping information through brochures, workshops, and demonstration projects. There is a $20 membership fee.

Native Plant Society of Oregon
1920 Engel Ave. N.W., Salem, OR 97304
585-9419
The society promotes knowledge and identification of Pacific Northwest native plants and protects Oregon's rare, threatened, and endangered plant species.

PLANT SOURCES
WILLAMETTE VALLEY
American Ornamental Perennial
P.O. Box 385, Gresham, OR 97030-0054
661-4836
Specializes in native grasses.

Dennis' 7 Dees
6025 S.E. Powell Blvd., Portland, OR 97206
777-1422
Has a special section just for native plants, at all three stores.

10445 S.W. Barnes Rd., Portland, OR 97225
297-1058

1090 McVey Ave., Lake Oswego, OR 97034
636-4660

Dragonfly Gardens
2230 S.E. Hawthorne Blvd., Portland, OR 97202
235-9150
Carries an extensive selection of flowers but no shrubbery.

Northwest Garden Spot
2635 N.W. Thurman St., Portland, OR 97210

274-2439
Carries a wide selection.

Portland Nursery
5050 S.E. Stark St., Portland, OR 97215
231-5050
Has a special section just for native plants.

Russell Graham Herbaceous Nursery
4030 Eagle Crest N.W., Salem, OR 97304
362-1135
This is a good place to find your native Oregon trees and shrubs.

SOUTHERN OREGON
Chet's Garden Center
229 S.W. H St., Grants Pass, OR 97526
276-4424
Has a small selection.

Siskiyou Rare Plant Nursery
2825 Cummings Rd., Medford, OR 97501
772-6846
Offers a good selection of native plants.

Forest Farm
990 Tetherow Rd., Williams, OR 97544
846-6963
According to expert Dale Shank, Forest Farm has the largest selection of native Oregon plants in the state.

MAIL ORDER:
Stonecrop Gardens
2037 S.W. Sixteenth Ave., Albany, OR 97321-1835
928-8652
Stonecrop Gardens offers hardy succulents and cacti wholesale and through mail order. If you want to visit the grounds, call first for an appointment.

Nurseries, Organic Plant

WILLAMETTE VALLEY

Garland Nursery
5470 N.E. Hwy. 20, Corvallis, OR 97330
753-6601
Carries some organic plants.

Down to Earth Farm and Garden
Fifth Ave. & Olive St., Eugene, OR 97402
342-6820
Some of the vegetable and herb starts are organic.

Northwoods Nursery
28696 S. Cramer Rd., Molalla, OR 97038
651-3737
Northwoods Nursery (retail and mail order) features fruit trees, hardy kiwis, bamboo, and exotic, flowering ornamentals such as the maypop passionflower and the pineapple guava. Although not certified organic (several years ago the nursery sprayed a tenacious patch of thistle), it relies on organic gardening techniques and grows disease-resistant varieties of plants and trees.

Northwoods Nursery is open from the middle of January to the end of October and has a free catalog. It gives tree seedlings to schools or nonprofit organizations interested in sponsoring a tree planting event. "We'd like to think of school children seeing the trees grow."

Dennis' 7 Dees
6025 S.W. Powell Blvd., Portland, OR 97206
777-1422
Carries vegetables and herbs organically grown by Oregon Tilth-certified growers, at all three stores.

10445 S.W. Barnes Rd., Portland, OR 97225
297-1058

1090 McVey Ave., Lake Oswego, OR 97034
636-4660

Dragonfly Gardens
2230 S.W. Hawthorne Blvd., Portland, OR 97202

235-9150

Besides offering organically grown herbs and vegetables, this garden shop is one of the few in the state that can claim 95 percent of its perennials are organic. It even stocks organically grown house plants.

Earth Mercantile
6345 S.W. Capitol Hwy., Portland, OR 97201
246-4935
All the house plants and herbs are organically grown.

Mary Lou Emerson's house plant booth
Portland Saturday Market
The Portland Saturday Market (under the west side of the Burnside Bridge) is open from March to Christmas. All the house plants in Mary Lou Emerson's booth are organically grown.

Jean's Herb Shop
2036 W. Burnside St., Portland, OR 97201
228-7861
Offers organic herb starts and dried herbs.

Northwest Garden Spot
2635 N.W. Thurman St., Portland, OR 97210
274-2439
Besides organic vegetable and herb starts, Northwest Garden Spot offers organically grown container vegetable gardens and annual flower arrangements. The owner, Carol Knox, teaches classes in chemical-free gardening through MLC Community School; for information call 280-5742.

People's Food Store
3029 S.E. Twenty-first Ave., Portland, OR 97214
232-9051
In season the store carries organic herb and vegetable starts.

Portland Nursery
5050 S.E. Stark St., Portland, OR 97215
231-5050
Carries herb and vegetable starts supplied by an Oregon Tilth-certified grower.

Guentner's Gardens
5780 Commercial St. S.E., Salem, OR 97306
585-7133
The vegetables are organically grown.

SOUTHERN OREGON
Ray's Garden Center
2265 Hwy. 66, Ashland, OR 97520
482-9561
Carries some organic vegetables and herbs.

Rising Sun Farm Organic Herbs
2300 Colestin Rd., Ashland, OR 97520
482-5392
Besides being sold at roadside stands, the farm's organic herbs can be shipped across the country.

Chet's Garden Center
229 S.W. H St., Grants Pass, OR 97526
476-4424
Carries both organic vegetable and herb plants.

Redwood Nursery
1290 Redwood Ave., Grants Pass, OR 97527
476-2642
On a customer's request the nursery will set aside organic plants to assure they are not sprayed with chemicals.

Radford's Altamont Nursery
3237 Maryland Ave., Klamath Falls, OR 97603
884-0669
The nursery is now looking for organic growers as suppliers.

MAIL ORDER:
Nichols Garden Nursery
1190 N. Pacific Hwy., Albany, OR 97321
928-9280
Nichols Garden Nursery ships organic herb plants from April 15 through June 5 and from September 10 until cold weather sets in.
Send for the free catalog.

Northwoods Nursery
28696 S. Cramer Rd., Molalla, OR 97038
651-3737

Features fruit trees, hardy kiwis, bamboo, and exotic ornamentals. Although not certified organic, it relies on organic gardening techniques and grows disease-resistant varieties of plants and trees. Northwoods Nursery's shipping season for plants is from January through May. Send for the free catalog.

OIL, REREFINED, see RECYCLED PRODUCTS

ORGANIC COMPOST, see SOIL AMENDMENTS, ORGANIC

ORGANIC FERTILIZERS, see SOIL AMENDMENTS, ORGANIC

ORGANIC GARDENERS, see GARDEN AND LAWN CARE

ORGANIC PLANTS, see NURSERIES

ORGANIC PRODUCE, see FOOD

ORGANIC SEEDS, see SEEDS

Paints and Stains, Nontoxic

Most paints, stains, and wood finishes contain crude oil, plastics, or petroleum, and these toxins affect people, plants, and animals. A Johns Hopkins University study found more than three hundred toxic chemicals in ordinary household paints.

Only a few companies make completely, or almost completely, nontoxic products. Auro and Livos, both produced in Germany, are two of the most environmentally safe products. They are made from pine resin, linseed oil, chalk, india rubber, and mineral-derived pigments. Of the commercially available paint products, water based are less toxic than oil based.

We were disappointed to find only one outlet in the entire state with a selection of paints and stains. Other stores should be encouraged to carry these products.

Down to Earth Home Shop
Fifth Ave. & Olive St., Eugene, OR 97401
344-6357
Down to Earth now has the Livos line of paints, stains, and varnishes.

Earth Mercantile
6344 S.W. Capitol Hwy., Portland, OR 97201
246-4935
Carries a natural organic varnish.

MAIL ORDER:
AFM Enterprises, Inc.
1140 Stacy Ct., Riverside, CA 92507
(714) 781-6860
AFM is one of the largest local manufacturers of nontoxic paint. Call for answers to technical questions or to find the outlet nearest you. AMF also manufactures sealers, enamels, cleaners, wax, stains, and carpet guard.

Baubiologie "Healthful" Hardware
207B Sixteenth St., Pacific Grove, CA 93950
(408) 372-8626
In addition to AFM Safecoat water-base enamel (ask for available color chips), the Baubiologie catalog has nontoxic concrete paint, primer, and a nonasbestos joint and patching compound; also various kinds of water seal for decks, bricks, or stucco, and adhesives.

EcoSource
9051 Mill Station Rd., Bldg. E, Sebastopol, CA 95472
(800) 688-8345
Besides the AFM line and CynoSeal products EcoSource carries nontoxic sealers and Leinos Citrus Thinner, a thinner made from citrus peels.

Nigra Enterprises
5699 Kanan Rd., Agoura, CA 91301
(818) 889-6877
Jim Nigra sells the AFM, Miller, and Pace Chem lines. The latter includes (besides safe paints) enamel, wood stain, primer undercoat, and a variety of adhesives and sealers. Nigra is hard to reach by phone, but we're told you're likely to be a satisfied customer when you do. Free consultations are offered, so the products you order will suit your needs.

Plant Chemistry
1365 Rufina Circle, Santa Fe, NM 87501
(800) 621-2591
Call for a catalog of the company's line of Livos paints, which includes natural resin paints in a wide variety of colors, water-based nontoxic paints, whitewash, and solvent-free paints, as well as a satin sheen enamel. The catalog also has nontoxic waxes, shellacs, wood glazes, adhesives, and cleaning products. The paint solvents available here do contain a synthetic from a crude-oil base; this is still less toxic than other solvents and does not emit a strong odor.

Seventh Generation
Colchester, VT 05446-1672
(800) 456-1177
Carries water-based, low-odor wood stains in maple, oak, or walnut; one quart, $13.95; two quarts, $26.95.

Sinan Co.
P.O. Box 857, Davis, CA 95617-0857
(916) 753-3104
Carries Auro paints and a number of nontoxic waxes, varnishes, lacquers, glues, and other natural building materials; request a catalog.

PAPER, RECYCLED

Note that some vendors of other kinds of recycled papers carry gift wrap and boxes from recycled fibers as well.

BOND, COMPUTER, WRITING, AND XEROGRAPHIC PAPERS

If you can't find a retail outlet in your area, check the Yellow Pages under Paper. Some of the paper distributors we have listed with Portland addresses, such as Unisource, Fraser, and Zellerbach, have local numbers or 800 numbers listed. These companies often require a minimum order.

STATEWIDE
Fred Meyer, Inc.
All Fred Meyer stores have a variety of recycled paper products (memo books, school supplies, copier paper, computer paper, scratch pads, fax sheets, and stationery), and they are expanding their lines.

WILLAMETTE VALLEY

SOS (Save Our ecoSystems, Inc.)
541 Willamette St. #102, Eugene, OR 97401
484-2679
The recycled office paper includes 100 percent recycled, nonsecondarily bleached bond paper and envelopes, by Earthtone. A brochure is available.

Earth Mercantile
6344 S.W. Capitol Hwy., Portland, OR 97201
246-4935
Carries both office supplies and personal stationery.

Ecology House
341 S.W. Morrison St., Portland, OR 97204
223-4883
Carries personal stationery plus recycled gift boxes and wrapping paper.

If Not Now...When?
512 N.W. Twenty-first Ave., Portland, OR 97209
222-4471
The stock includes a wide selection of recycled paper products for both personal and office use—everything from computer paper to recycled message pads.

Peacetree
1735 S.E. Madison St. #2, Portland, OR 97214
230-0436
Peacetree has a great selection, but some products might need to be ordered. Delivery is free for orders over $25, and for nonprofit groups discounts are available.

People's Food Store
3029 S.E. Twenty-first Ave., Portland, OR 97214
232-9051
Carries recycled personal stationery products.

SOUTHERN OREGON

Crater Paper Co.
9 E. Fourth St., Medford, OR 97201
452-8900

Carries recycled copier, computer, and printing paper.

THE COAST
The Community Store, Inc.
1389 Duane St., Astoria, OR 97103
325-0027

The Naturalist
587 Pacific Way, Gearhart, OR 97138
738-8934

Oceana Co-op Natural Foods
415 N.W. Coast St., Newport, OR 97365
265-8285

DISTRIBUTORS:
These distributors will sell recycled paper to you or your printer. Some of them have a minimum, which might exceed the cost of your purchase; direct your printer to them, for the papers you want to use.

Northwest Resource Recycling
1680-A Irving Rd., Eugene, OR 97402
461-2000

SOS (Save Our eco-Systems, Inc.)
407 Blair Blvd., Eugene, OR 97402
484-2679
Contact Barbara Kelley.

The Unisource Corp.
2690 S.E. Mailwell Dr., Milwaukie, OR 97222
654-6560
Contact Ernie Blather.
Unisource also has an outlet in Medford (772-2610).

AJP
1120 S.E. Morrison St., Portland, OR 97204
235-8341
Contact Jeb Boyer.

Barber-Ellis Paper Co.
2619 N.W. Industrial Way, Portland, OR 97210
227-3372
Contact Stewart Hestor.

Fraser Paper Co.
3551 N.W. Yeon Ave., Portland, OR 97210
227-6000
Contact Bobby Cupto.

Peacetree Recycled Paper
1735 S.E. Madison St. #2, Portland, OR 97214
230-0436

Service Paper Co.
1705 N.E. Argyle St., Portland, OR 97211
285-7516
Contact Nancy Gruse.

Supplyways, Inc.
4600 N.W. St. Helens Rd., Portland, OR 97210
288-6561
Contact Mary Jackson.

Western Paper Co.
6000 N. Cutter Circle, Portland, OR 97217
289-2800
Contact Tony Montes.

Zellerbach Paper Co.
9111 N.E. Columbia Blvd., Portland, OR 97220
256-6612
Contact Jeff Martine.

MAIL ORDER:
Conservatree Paper Co.
10 Lombard St. #250, San Francisco, CA 94111
(800) 522-9200
One of the largest distributors of office and printing papers, Conservatree sells by carton only, with a $100 minimum purchase. This company can tell you who manufactures what.

Earth Care Paper, Inc.
P.O. Box 3335, Dept. 99, Madison, WI 53704
(608) 256-5522
Carries printing, copier, and computer papers; gift wrap; greeting cards; and stationery. A free catalog includes samples.

Ecco Bella
6 Provost Sq. #602, Caldwell, NJ 07006
(201) 226-5799
Carries computer and high-speed copier papers; envelopes; 100 percent recycled, unbleached printing and writing papers; and note cards and wrapping paper.

Eco Solutions
1929 S. Fifth St., Minneapolis, MN 55454
(612) 338-0250
Small orders are welcome here for the large selection of computer and office papers. Other paper products include Envision products—100 percent recycled toilet paper, facial tissues, dinner napkins, and paper towels packaged in paper.

EcoSource
9051 Mill Station Rd., Bldg. E, Sebastopol, CA 95472
(800) 688-8345
C-100 is EcoSource's most environmentally sound paper. It's 100 percent recycled, and you can order envelopes and computer, copier, letterhead, and printing papers in either white or natural.

Graham-Pierce
P.O. Box 1866, Fairview Heights, IL 62208
(800) 851-3899
Besides carrying printing papers, Graham-Pierce prints letterhead, envelopes, business cards, brochures, and newsletters on a variety of recycled papers.

Recycled Paper Company, Inc.
185 Corey Rd., Boston, MA 02146
(617) 277-9901
Small-quantity purchases can be made (and free samples are given) of printing, copier, and computer papers and stationery and envelopes.

Recycled Paper Outlet
P.O. Box 66241, Portland, OR 97266
760-8445
Carries office papers with envelopes, and offers free samples.

INDUSTRIAL PAPER
DISTRIBUTORS:
Scot Supply
1464 W. Sixth Ave., Eugene, OR 97402
342-5473

Concannon's Portland Paper
3313 N.W. Guam Ave., Portland, OR 97210
243-6816
Contact Mark Huddleston.

Pope & Talbot
1500 S.W. First Ave., Portland, OR 97201
228-1961
Contact Greg Sullivan.

Service Paper Co.
1795 N.E. Argyle St., Portland, OR 97211
285-7516
Contact Pat Buck.

Western Paper Co.
6000 N. Cutter Circle, Portland, OR 97217
289-2800
Contact Tony Montes.

Zellerbach Paper Co.
9111 N.E. Columbia Blvd., Portland, OR 97220
255-2121

PAPER MILLS

These companies sell to distributors or printers. Call them for information, samples, and names of local suppliers for you or your printer.

Ashdun Industries, Inc.
1605 John St., Fort Lee, NJ 07024
(800) 447-3008
Manufactures C.A.R.E. Paper Products (Consumer Action to Restore the Environment): recycled toilet paper, paper towels, tissues, and more.

Cross Pointe Paper Corp.
2625 Butterfield Rd., 2301N, Oak Brook, IL 60521
(800) 543-3297
Manufactures recycled writing, printing, and copier papers; stocks book- and magazine-publishing grades.

Eastern Fine Paper
P.O. Box 129, Brewer, ME 04412
(800) 341-1750
Manufactures writing, offset, mimeograph, and high-speed copier papers.

Fox River Paper Co.
P.O. Box 2215, Appleton, WI 54913
(414) 733-7341
Manufactures printing and writing papers. The cotton fiber papers are made from recovered material.

French Paper Co.
100 French St., Box 398, Niles, MI 49120
(616) 683-1100
Manufactures book papers, cover stock, and specialty papers.

George Whiting Paper Co.
P.O. Box 28, Menasha, WI 54952
(414) 722-3351
Manufacturers 80 percent-recycled printing paper, and takes special orders.

Georgia-Pacific Corp.
P.O. Box 105605, Atlanta, GA 30348-5605
(404) 521-6265
Manufactures offset, computer, and carbonless papers and office forms.

Hyde Park Paper
892 River St., Hyde Park, MA 02138
(617) 361-3500
Manufactures printing and high-speed copier papers, and book and cover stock.

P.H. Glatfelter Co.
228 S. Main St., Spring Grove, PA 17362
(717) 225-4711
Manufactures printing, writing, and office papers; some are 100 percent recycled.

Riverside Paper Co.
800 S. Lawe St., Appleton, WI 54915
(414) 733-5546
Manufactures printing, typing, and copier papers.

Simpson Paper Co.
100 N. Erie St., Box 2648, Pomona, CA 91766
(714) 835-7401
Manufactures high-speed copier paper that is 50 percent recycled.

TOILET PAPER, PAPER TOWELS, AND FACIAL TISSUES

You can now find household paper products (toilet paper, paper towels, paper napkins, facial tissue, coffee filters, and feminine hygiene products) made from recycled paper in many supermarkets and health food stores. Make a point of adding them to your standard grocery list.

STATEWIDE
Cub Foods

Fred Meyer, Inc.
All stores carry 100 percent dioxin-free coffee filters (Melitta and Natural Brew) and 100 percent recycled, nonsecondarily bleached toilet paper, paper towels, and facial tissue (Today's Choice).

Safeway Stores
All stores carry 100 percent recycled, nonsecondarily bleached toilet paper, napkins, paper towels, coffee filters, and facial tissue (Care).

WILLAMETTE VALLEY

First Alternative
1007 S.E. Third Ave., Corvallis, OR 97333
753-3115
Carries the Envision line.

Sunshine General Store
824 W. Main St., Cottage Grove, OR 97424
942-8836
Carries toilet paper and paper towels from recycled fibers.

Food Value
2102 Bailey Hill Rd., Eugene, OR 97405
686-1821
Carries toilet paper, paper towels, and facial tissue from recycled fibers at all four stores.

2858 Willamette St., Eugene, OR 97405
342-5779

1960 Franklin Blvd., Eugene, OR 97403
343-6418

2750 River Rd., Eugene, OR 97404
688-0555

Fredrick's Food Warehouse
2025 River Rd., Eugene, OR 97404
688-1467
Carries a variety of paper products from recycled fibers.

Friendly Foods and Deli
2757 Friendly St., Eugene, OR 97405
683-2079
Carries Envision and Green Forest paper towels, toilet paper, facial tissue, napkins, and feminine products, all dioxin free.

Kiva
125 W. Eleventh Ave., Eugene, OR 97401
342-8666
Carries the Envision line.

New Frontier Market
Eighth Ave. & Van Buren St., Eugene, OR 97502
345-7401
Carries the Envision line.

Oasis
2489 Willamette St., Eugene, OR 97405
345-1014
Carries Envision and H-Dry products.

Red Barn Grocery
357-A Van Buren St., Eugene, OR 97402
342-7503
Carries Envision paper products.

Sundance
748 E. Twenty-fourth Ave., Eugene, OR 97401
345-0141
Carries Envision toilet paper, paper towels, and facial tissue.

Daily Grind
4026 S.E. Hawthorne Blvd., Portland, OR 97214
223-5521
Carries toilet paper and paper towels from recycled fibers.

Earth Mercantile
6344 S.W. Capitol Hwy., Portland, OR 97201
246-4935
Carries the entire line of Envision products.

Ecology House
341 S.W. Morrison St., Portland, OR 97204
223-4883
Carries toilet paper and paper towels from recycled fibers.

Food Front Co-op Grocery
2375 N.W. Thurman St., Portland, OR 97210
222-5658
Carries toilet paper, tissue, and paper towels from recycled fibers, and gives $.05 back for paper bags.

Happy Harvest Grocery
2348 S.E. Ankeny St., Portland, OR 97214
235-5358
Carries toilet paper, paper towels, and facial tissue from recycled fibers.

If Not Now...When?
512 N.W. Twenty-first Ave., Portland, OR 97209
222-4471
Carries toilet paper, paper towels, facial tissue, and napkins from recycled fibers.

Nature's Fresh Northwest
5909 S.W. Corbett St., Portland, OR 97219
244-3934
Carries toilet paper, paper towels, and facial tissue from recycled fibers at all four stores.

3449 N.E. Twenty-fourth Ave., Portland, OR 97212
288-3414

6344 S.W. Capitol Hwy., Portland, OR 97225
244-3110

4000 S.W. 117th Ave., Beaverton, OR 97005
646-3824

People's Food Store
3029 S.E. Twenty-first Ave., Portland, OR 97214
232-9051
Carries Envision and Park Avenue toilet paper.

Heliotrope Natural Foods
2060 Market St. N.E., Salem, OR 97301
362-5487
Carries toilet paper, paper towels, and facial tissue from recycled fibers.

Perrywinkle Provisions
1101 Main St., Sweet Home, OR 97386
367-6614
Carries the Green Forest and Envision lines.

SOUTHERN OREGON

Ashland Community Food Store
37 Third St., Ashland, OR 97520
482-2237
Carries toilet paper and paper towels from recycled fibers.

Promise Natural Food Store
503 S. Main St., Canyonville, OR 97417
839-4167
Carries paper towels and toilet paper from recycled fibers.

Hammer's Model Market
202 S. Redwood Hwy., Cave Junction, OR 97523
592-3236
Carries Envision, Green Forest, and Enviro paper products.

Dee's Market
4601 Carnes Rd., Roseburg, OR 97470
679-7771
Carries toilet paper, paper towels, napkins, and facial tissue from recycled fibers at all four stores.

930 W. Harvard Blvd., Roseburg, OR 97470
673-8060

811 E. Central St., Sutherlin, OR 97479
459-2697

Hwy. 42, Winston, OR 97496
679-4028

New Day Quality
210 S.E. Jackson St., Roseburg, OR 97470
672-0275
Carries Envision paper products.

EASTERN AND CENTRAL OREGON

Nature's General Store
Wagner Mall, Bend, OR 97702
382-6732
Carries Envision products.

Wy' East
110 Eighth St., Hood River, OR 97031
386-6181
Carries paper towels and toilet paper from recycled fibers.

Oregon Natural Market
340 S.W. Fifth St., Ontario, OR 97914
889-8714
Carries toilet paper from recycled fibers.

Apple Jack's
110 S. Spruce St., Sisters, OR 97759
549-5781
Carries paper towels and toilet paper from recycled fibers.

THE COAST

The Community Store, Inc.
1389 Duane St., Astoria, OR 97103
325-0027
Carries paper towels, toilet paper, and facial tissue from recycled fibers.

Generous Helpings
604 Spruce St., Brookings, OR 97415
469-5414
Carries paper towels and toilet paper from recycled fibers.

Osburn's Grocery & Deli
240 N. Hemlock St., Cannon Beach, OR 97110
436-2234
Carries paper towels and toilet paper from recycled fibers.

Nosler's Natural Grocery
99 E. First St., Coquille, OR 97423
396-4823
Carries the Envision line.

Trillium Natural Grocery
1026 S.E. Jetty Ave., Lincoln City, OR 97367
994-5665
Carries paper towels and toilet paper from recycled fibers.

Oceana Co-op Natural Foods
415 N.W. Coast St., Newport, OR 97365
265-8285
Carries paper towels, toilet paper, and facial tissue from recycled fibers.

Coos Head Food Store
1960 Sherman Ave., North Bend, OR 97459
756-7264
Carries Envision paper products.

Grady's Market
580 N.E. Broadway, Waldport, OR 97394
563-3542
Carries paper towels, toilet paper, and facial tissue from recycled fibers.

MAIL ORDER:
Mail-order companies ship a variety of paper products, making it easy for all of us to switch over to recycled paper goods.

Brush Dance
218 Cleveland Ct., Mill Valley, CA 94941
(415) 389-6228
Carries recycled wrapping paper and greeting cards.

Co-op America
c/o Order Service
10 Farrell St., South Burlington, VT 05403
(800) 456-1177
Carries unperforated plain brown kraft paper in 400-foot rolls, facial tissues, kitchen towels, bathroom tissues, and cellulose food bags (which contain no plastics).

Eco Solutions
1929 S. Fifth St., Minneapolis, MN 55454
(612) 338-0250
Small orders are welcome here for the large selection of computer and office papers. Other paper products include Envision products—100 percent recycled toilet paper, facial tissues, dinner napkins, and paper towels packaged in paper.

Seventh Generation
Colchester, VT 05446-1672
(800) 456-1177
The Envision products sold include 100 percent recycled toilet paper, facial tissues, dinner napkins, and paper towels; stationery, wrapping paper, note paper, journals, and ruled pads; cellulose sandwich, freezer, and food-storage bags that totally disintegrate; paper trash bags; and paper plates made from 100 percent recycled paper.

Solar Electric
116 Fourth St., Santa Rosa, CA 95401
(800) 832-1986, (707) 542-1900
Fax (707) 542-4358
"Natural Brew" filters are made with unbleached paper for a dioxin-free cup of coffee; one hundred eight-inch fluted filters for $1.95. Also dinner napkins, toilet paper, facial tissue, and paper towels from Envision.

PAPER TRASH BAGS, see BAGS

PARK AND RIDE, see PUBLIC TRANSPORTATION

PEST CONTROL, SAFE

BENEFICIAL ORGANISMS

"Beneficials" are the good bugs, the ones that feed on the bugs that eat your fruits and vegetables. Remember they don't know one yard from the next, and they will move on when their food supply of pests dwindles. Also beneficials can be killed off by your neighbor's pesticides. You may need to replace them from time to time. And you may want to talk with your neighbors about a community-based nontoxic pest control program.

In addition to the sources listed below for Oregon and for mail orders, there is a free booklet (one per request) that lists all the suppliers of beneficial organisms in North America; at last count there were sixty. It's published by the California Department of Food and Agriculture:

Biological Control Services Program
3288 Meadowview Rd., Sacramento, CA 95832
(916) 427-4590

STATEWIDE

Fred Meyer, Inc.
All Fred Meyer garden stores carry ladybugs and praying mantises.

WILLAMETTE VALLEY

Vollstedt's Green Thumb
410 Pacific Blvd. S.W., Albany, OR 97321
928-2521
Carries ladybugs and praying mantises.

Garland Nursery
5470 N.E. Hwy. 20, Corvallis, OR 97330
753-6601
Carries ladybugs.

Down to Earth Farm and Garden
Fifth Ave. & Olive St., Eugene, OR 97402
342-6820
Down to Earth will special-order bugs including green lacewing larvae and predatory mites.

Gray's Garden Shop
737 W. Sixth Ave., Eugene, OR 97402
345-1569
Both stores carry ladybugs and praying mantises.

444 E. Main St., Springfield, OR 97478
747-2301

Oregon Garden Store
333 S. State St., Lake Oswego, OR 97034
697-3635
Carries ladybugs and praying mantises.

Dennis' 7 Dees
6025 S.E. Powell Blvd., Portland, OR 97206
777-1422
All three stores carry a wide variety of beneficial organisms in season. You might also check the store's reference book *Willamette Garden Guide* to find out how companion growing can eliminate pests. Dennis' 7 Dees

has just started carrying Predfeed, an organic substance that attracts ladybugs and other beneficials.

10445 S.W. Barnes Rd., Portland, OR 97225
297-1058

1090 McVey Ave., Lake Oswego, OR 97034
636-4660

Dragonfly Gardens
2230 S.E. Hawthorne Blvd., Portland, OR 97202
235-9150
Carries ladybugs, praying mantises, and beneficial nematodes.

Drake's 7 Dees
16519 S.E. Stark St., Portland, OR 97233
255-9225
Carries ladybugs and praying mantises.

Northwest Garden Spot
2635 N.W. Thurman St., Portland, OR 97210
274-2439
Carries ladybugs, praying mantises, and beneficial nematodes.

Portland Nursery
5050 S.E. Stark St., Portland, OR 97215
231-5050
Carries a large variety of bugs in season.

Guentner's Gardens
5780 Commercial St. S.E., Salem, OR 97306
585-7133
Carries ladybugs and praying mantises.

SOUTHERN OREGON
Ray's Garden Center
2265 Hwy. 66, Ashland, OR 97520
482-9561
Carries ladybugs and praying mantises.

Chet's Garden Center
229 S.W. H St., Grants Pass, OR 97526
476-4424
Carries ladybugs and praying mantises.

Redwood Nursery
1290 Redwood Ave., Grants Pass, OR 97527
476-2642
Carries ladybugs and praying mantises—and can stock others within twenty-four hours.

EASTERN AND CENTRAL OREGON

Redmond's Greenhouse
4101 S. Hwy. 97, Redmond, OR 97756
548-5418
Carries ladybugs.

THE COAST

Sandy's Nursery and Garden Center
3800 Hwy. 101 N., Tillamook, OR 97141
842-7270
Carries ladybugs.

MAIL ORDER:

We've seen little boxes of ladybugs and praying mantises in a number of hardware stores, nurseries, and home-improvement stores. But if the stores in your area are out, or if you want other kinds of beneficials to add to your garden, along with lots of specific information, you may want to call one of these companies.

Baubiologie "Healthful" Hardware
207B Sixteenth St., Pacific Grove, CA 93950
(408) 372-8626
Baubiologie carries green lacewings, which eat aphids, citrus mealybugs, spider mites, and a host of other pests; trichogramma wasps, parasites that eat pest worm and caterpillar eggs; fly parasites; and praying mantises, which have a varied diet. It offers a garden pack with a little of each, plus five hundred earthworms to aerate your soil.

Foothill Agricultural Research
510 W. Chase Dr., Corona, CA 91720
(714) 371-0120

This company carries insects that help control red scale, white ash fly, aphids, and much more. It also sells decollate snails, predator snails that eat common garden snail eggs and small snails, leaving only the large ones for you to collect. Within a year or two they'll control all your garden snails.

Gardens Alive!
Natural Gardening Research Center
Hwy. 48, Box 149, Sunman, IN 47041
(812) 623-3800

Among the many products here you'll find Gnatrol, which kills fungus gnats in gardens and house plants; BugPro and Haven flowering herbs, which attract beneficial insects; green lacewings and ladybugs, which eat aphids and other nuisances; trichogramma wasps, parasites that attack the eggs of more than two hundred garden pests; and praying mantises.

J. Harold Mitchell Co.
305 Agostino Rd., San Gabriel, CA 91776
(213) 287-1101

All the Mitchell Co. sells is decollate snails, which eat the pesky garden variety; $25 per hundred.

Peaceful Valley Farm Supply
P.O. Box 2209, Grass Valley, CA 95945
(916) 272-4769

Peaceful Valley sells a slew of beneficial organisms; its catalog tells you just what each one feeds on, how many you need, and when to release them (you don't just open the box and say "Fetch!"). Trichogramma wasps, beneficial mites, nematodes, decollate snails—you name 'em, they probably have 'em in stock. They also sell a mousetrap that allows you to insert a cracker barrier that the caught critter can chew through, to escape the trap wherever you've moved it.

Bargyla Rateaver, Ph.D.
9049 Covina St., San Diego, CA 92126
(619) 566-8994

Pest nematodes are tiny worms that stunt plant growth; yellow leaves and low crop yields are characteristic of its damage. A number of favorite vegetables, like carrots and tomatoes, are particularly vulnerable to them. Dr. Rateaver has a mixture of spores from fungi that do deadly things to these nematodes.

Sespe Creek Insectary
1400 Grand Ave., Fillmore, CA 93015
(805) 524-3565
In addition to parasite wasps for California red scale ($1 per thousand), scale-feeding black ladybugs (call for the price), tent traps, and the California red scale pheromone lures that give off an irresistible odor to red scale, the insectary has decollate snails ($7 for a hundred). These are the predator snails that gobble up brown-snail eggs and little tender brown snails. The big guys know enough to run from decollates, but the predator snails control the brown snails' population so they can't eat everything in sight.

Solar Electric
116 Fourth St., Santa Rosa, CA 95401
(800) 832-1986, (707) 542-1900
Fax (707) 542-4358
BioSafe Biological Lawn & Garden Insect Control is a broad-based organic insecticide that uses the species *Steinernema carpocapsae* to control soil-dwelling insects. Solar Electric also sells ladybugs and a sonic stake named GOPHER IT that drives away burrowing rodents without traps, gases, or poisons.

Territorial Seed Company
P.O. Box 157, Cottage, OR 97424
942-9547
Carries trichogramma wasps, green lacewing larvae, and BioSafe.

EXTERMINATORS

The following two exterminators may use some pesticides but are committed to employing natural mortality factors whenever possible. Addresses are not listed because the companies use referral call lines. One office is used for several outlets, but the customer does not pay a long-distance charge. For more information about pesticides contact ASQE or NCAP:

ASQE (Association for Safety and Quality in Extermination)
Brandon Ham

(800) 633-6041, Portland 652-7652

Anyone in the country can call the toll-free number above for pesticide information. Brandon Ham, who has been answering the ASQE line since 1987, gives seminars on pesticides and testifies in lawsuits as an expert witness. He also stays in touch with scientists studying pesticides across the country, and if material exists on a pesticide you want to know about, he will send you printed data sheets.

Brandon warns, "How a pesticide is applied can be as important as what pesticide is used." Ask your exterminator for details. No pesticide is applied in its pure form, and the accompanying nontargeting chemicals may be extremely harmful.

NCAP (Northwest Coalition for Alternatives to Pesticides)
P.O. Box 1393, Eugene, OR 97440
344-5044

If you want organic alternatives, if you want to become politically active in reducing pesticides, if you have been harmed by chemicals, contact NCAP.

NCAP recommends that you ask the following questions about any pesticide:

- What are the hazards for the occupants, the pets, and the environment?
- How effective is it? (The government will register a pesticide for use without evidence of its efficiency.)
- Is the pesticide still effective, or have pests become resistant to it?
- Is it quick acting, or slow acting and longer lasting?
- Is it repellent as applied to the pest that you have?
- How much will the active ingredient cost per volume?
- Is your exterminator aware whether anyone in your household is pregnant, chemically sensitive, asthmatic, less than one year old, or elderly?

Killer Inc.

In 1982 when a customer's family had to move from their home because of harsh chemicals, Killer Inc. made a commitment to use environmentally safe alternatives. It spearheaded an Oregon law banning chlordane as a pesticide and now would like to see dursban, which it believes to be equally dangerous, outlawed. Whenever possible Killer Inc. uses biological methods rather than chemicals. With partial funding from the Environmental Learning Center at Clackamas Community College it found methods for using nematodes to eliminate termite nests.

Ladybug Pest Eliminators, Inc.
Ladybug Pest Eliminators has also made a commitment to use environmentally safe alternatives.

WILLAMETTE VALLEY
Killer Inc.: Eugene
461-0558

Killer Inc.: Northeast and North Portland
284-2555

Ladybug Pest Eliminators, Inc.: North and East Portland, and Gresham
775-0006

Killer Inc.: Southeast Portland and Gresham
775-6878

Killer Inc.: Milwaukie, Oregon City, and Lake Oswego
656-6262

Ladybug Pest Eliminators, Inc.: Milwaukie, Oregon City, and Lake Oswego
656-0182

Killer Inc.: Northwest and Southwest Portland, Beaverton, and Tigard
626-6262, 245-5544

Ladybug Pest Eliminators, Inc.: Southwest Portland, Beaverton, and Tigard
245-9423

Killer Inc.: Metro West and Aloha
649-4747

Killer Inc.: Salem
364-8091

SOUTHERN OREGON
Killer Inc.: Grants Pass
474-1119

Killer Inc.: Klamath Falls
883-5295

Killer Inc.: Medford
772-2687

Killer Inc.: Phoenix
535-4355

Killer Inc.: Roseburg
673-9854

THE COAST
Killer Inc.: Astoria
325-0162

Killer Inc.: Lincoln City
994-6227

Killer Inc.: Newport
265-6813

Killer Inc.: Tillamook
842-2818

PESTICIDES AND INSECTICIDES
STATEWIDE
Fred Meyer, Inc.
All the Fred Meyer garden shops carry the complete Safer line.

WILLAMETTE VALLEY
Vollstedt's Green Thumb
410 Pacific Blvd. S.W., Albany, OR 97321
928-2521
   Besides the complete Safer line, Vollstedt's has BT and pyrethrum for both indoor and outdoor use.

Garland Nursery
5470 N.E. Hwy. 20, Corvallis, OR 97330
753-6601

Carries the complete Safer line, and plans to expand its organic pesticides.

Down to Earth Farm and Garden
Fifth Ave. & Olive St., Eugene, OR 97402
342-6820
Besides the store's own diatomaceous earth it carries Safer, BioSafe, Bonide, Whitmore Labs, and Pratt products. This store supplies only organic solutions, so the staff's knowledge is comprehensive.

Gray's Garden Shop
737 W. Sixth Ave., Eugene, OR 97402
345-1569
Carries Safer and Bonide products at both stores.

444 E. Main St., Springfield, OR 97478
747-2301

Oregon Garden Store
333 S. State St., Lake Oswego, OR 97034
697-3635
Carries Safer products, beneficial nematodes, and BT.

Northwoods Nursery
28696 S. Cramer Rd., Molalla, OR 97038
651-3737
Northwoods Nursery is open from the middle of January to the end of October. It carries Safer products, Red Arrow, *bacillus thuringiensis* (BT, the bacteria that eat the insides of insects), pyrethrum, microcop, sulfur, lime sulfur, and fish oil as a dormant spray. Northwoods Nursery also has Bio-Lure bug traps for apple maggot, codling moth, cherry fruit fly, and walnut husk fly. If deer are nibbling in your garden, try their organic Deer Away.

Dennis' 7 Dees
6025 S.E. Powell Blvd., Portland, OR 97206
777-1422
Besides the complete Safer line all stores have diatomaceous earth, which controls slugs and soft-bodied insects while amending soil; beneficial nematodes and BT; also tobacco dust, sulfur, and Bonide products. The

stores recommend their vibrating bird lines, pheromone traps, and slug traps. Tell them your problem and they can give you a safe solution.

10445 S.W. Barnes Rd., Portland, OR 97225
297-1058

1090 McVey Ave., Lake Oswego, OR 97034
636-4660

Dragonfly Gardens
2230 S.E. Hawthorne Blvd., Portland, OR 97202
235-9150
In organic pesticides Dragonfly Gardens carries the Black Leaf, Red Arrow, and Cook lines. It also has diatomaceous earth (in bins), beneficial nematodes, and BT.

Drake's 7 Dees
16519 S.E. Stark St., Portland, OR 97233
255-9225
Carries the complete line of Safer products.

Earth Mercantile
6345 S.W. Capitol Hwy., Portland, OR 97201
246-4935
Besides the Safer line Earth Mercantile carries a safe mosquito repellent and sells diatomaceous earth with a mitt for flea control.

If Not Now...When?
512 N.W. Twenty-first Ave., Portland, OR 97201
222-4471
Carries the Safer line.

Northwest Garden Spot
2635 N.W. Thurman St., Portland, OR 97210
274-2439
Carries Safer and Ringer products and also pyrethrum, BT, and oyster shells (in bins), a slug deterrent.

Portland Nursery
5050 S.E. Stark St., Portland, OR 97215

231-5050
Carries the complete Safer line of products, tobacco dust, sulfur, BT, diatomaceous earth, and beneficial nematodes.

Guentner's Gardens
5780 Commercial St. S.E., Salem, OR 97306
585-7133
Carries nicotine by Black Leaf and the complete Safer line.

SOUTHERN OREGON

Ray's Garden Center
2265 Hwy. 66, Ashland, OR 97520
482-9561
Carries the complete Safer line.

Chet's Garden Center
229 S.W. H St., Grants Pass, OR 97526
476-4424
Carries the complete Safer line, for both garden and pets, and BT.

Redwood Nursery
1290 Redwood Ave., Grants Pass, OR 97527
476-2642
Carries Safer and Pratt Science products.

Radford's Altamont Nursery
3237 Maryland Ave., Klamath Falls, OR 97603
884-0669
Carries Safer insecticidal soap and BT, and plans to expand this section of the nursery. For cold Klamath winters Radford's carries Frost Guard—replicating bacteria that protect against frost.

EASTERN AND CENTRAL OREGON

Landsystems
21336 Hwy. 20 E., Bend, OR 97701
389-5926
Carries Ringer and Safer products.

Redmond's Greenhouse
4101 S. Hwy. 97, Redmond, OR 97756

548-5418
Carries Bonide and Safer products.

THE COAST
Raintree Garden and Gift
Hamlet Rt. Box 304, Seaside, OR 97138
738-6980
Carries Safer products.

MAIL ORDER:
Nichols Garden Nursery
1190 N. Pacific Hwy., Albany, OR 97321
928-9280
Carries BT, 100 percent pyrethrum powder, rotenone, Red Arrow, and slug and housefly traps.

Territorial Seed Company
P.O. Box 157, Cottage, OR 97424
942-9547
Carries Dipel (contains BT), liquid rotenone and pyrethrum, tobacco dust, Safer soap, Cuke and Melon Dust, diatomaceous earth, and insect traps.

Northwoods Nursery
28696 S. Cramer Rd., Molalla, OR 97038
651-3737
Carries Safer products, BT, pyrethrum, Red Arrow, microcop, sulfur, lime sulfur, and fish oil as a dormant spray. Northwoods Nursery has Bio-Lure bug traps for apple maggot, codling moth, cherry fruit fly, and walnut husk fly. It also carries Deer Away, an organic deer repellent.

PESTICIDES, see PEST CONTROL

PHOTOVOLTAICS, see SOLAR ENERGY

POLLUTION COMPLAINTS

Oregon has many agencies that respond to pollution complaints. The Department of Environmental Quality has offices in seven areas of the state (they're listed below); for specialized problems see the table of agencies to call. For example, if you see a smoking auto call in a complaint to the DMV, which will ask your name and the license number of the auto, date you observed it, and the location. After a computer search it will send a notice to the address of the owner saying that the car is in violation of Oregon clean air laws and the violation must be rectified in thirty days. Your name is not included in the notice.

State Agencies to Call with Pollution Complaints

FOR COMPLAINTS INVOLVING	CALL
Crop damage	Oregon Department of Agriculture (ODA): 378-3773
Drinking water	Oregon Division of Health (ODH): 229-5821
	Pesticide Analytic and Response Center (PARC): 378-3793
Human health	Oregon Accident Prevention Division (APD): 800-922-2689
	PARC: 378-3793
	Oregon Department of Health (ODH): 229-5851
Irrigation water	Department of Environmental Quality (DEQ): see phone numbers below, by region.
Label violations	Oregon Department of Agriculture: 378-3773
Pollution complaints	Department of Environmental Quality: see phone numbers below, by region.
Smoking automobiles	Department of Motor Vehicles (DMV): statewide (800) 452-4011; Portland 229-6238
Spills	Oregon Accident Response System (OARS): (800) 452-0311
	DEQ: see numbers below, by region.
Wildlife and fish	Oregon Department of Fish and Wildlife (ODFW), Habitat Conservation Division:

229-6732
PARC: 378-3793

DEQ REGIONAL OFFICES

If you know of industrial or residential pollution violations (someone in your neighborhood dumping hazardous waste in a drain, for instance), you can file a complaint with the DEQ through your regional office. Inspectors are dispatched to investigate.

Anonymous calls are rarely taken, unless there is corroborative evidence or a history of prior complaints. The department takes your name but can do so under a seal of confidentiality. Names are taken for two reasons: to prevent the harassment of one neighbor by another and for use in case the inspector gets lost.

In 1989 the DEQ received three thousand pollution complaint calls. The department expects the number to increase.

Central Region
2146 N.E. Fourth St., Bend, OR 97701
388-6146
Serves Crook, Deschutes, Harney, Hood River, Jefferson, Klamath, Lake, Sherman, and Wasco counties.

Coos Bay Branch
490 N. Second St., Coos Bay, OR 97701
388-6146
Serves Coos and Curry counties.

Eastern Region
700 S.E. Emigrant St., Pendleton, OR 97801
276-4063
Serves Baker, Gilliam, Grant, Malheur, Morrow, Umatilla, Union, Wallowa, and Wheeler counties.

Northwest Region
811 S.W. Sixth Ave., Portland, OR 97204
229-5263
Serves Clackamas, Clatsop, Columbia, Multnomah, Tillamook, and Washington counties.

Roseburg Branch
1937 W. Harvard Blvd., Roseburg, OR 97470
440-3338
Serves Douglas County.

Southwest Region
201 W. Main St., Ste. 2-D, Medford, OR 97501
776-6010
Serves Douglas, Jackson, and Josephine counties.

Willamette Valley Region
895 Summer St. N.E., Salem, OR 97310
378-8240
Serves Benton, Lane, Lincoln, Linn, Marion, Polk, and Yamhill counties.

*P*RINTERS USING RECYCLED PAPER

Most printers will be happy to print on recycled papers and can get the paper for you quickly. Others say it's too hard to get, or they could get it but the minimum order is too expensive. The printers listed here specialize in working with recycled paper products.

Watermark Press
1123 S.E. Market St., Portland, OR 97214
233-6971
Contact Leslie Cowley.

Meridian Printing Co.
19365 S.W. Eighty-ninth Ave., Tualatin, OR 97062
692-0905
Contact Chuck Hale.

Print Right
27375 S.W. Parkway Ave., Wilsonville, OR 97070
682-1322

*P*UBLICATIONS

ENERGY CONSERVATION AND ALTERNATIVE SOURCES

Fact sheets available from:

CAREIRS (Conservation and Renewable Energy Inquiry and Referral Service)
P.O. Box 8900, Silver Spring, MD 20907
(800) 523-2929
Free fact sheets on energy conservation and other subjects: photovoltaics, landscaping for energy-efficient homes, improving the energy-efficiency of windows, solar energy and your home, energy-efficient lighting, solar-energy systems consumer tips, and much more.

The Most Energy-Efficient Appliances available from:
American Council for an Energy-Efficient Economy
1001 Connecticut Ave. N.W. #535, Washington, DC 20036
(202) 429-8873
An annual listing of the top-rated residential equipment on the U.S. market; $2.

The New Solar Home, by Joel Davidson
Culver City: Davidson Co., 1987. $21.95, available from:
Davidson Co.
P.O. Box 4126, Culver City, CA 90231
(213) 202-7882
More than four hundred pages of information on photovoltaics; comes with a money-back guarantee.

Saving Energy and Money with Home Appliances available from:
American Council for an Energy-Efficient Economy
1001 Connecticut Ave. N.W. #535, Washington, DC 20036
(202) 429-8873
Facts on which home appliances are energy conserving and which are not; $2.

The Smart Kitchen: How to Design a Comfortable, Safe, Energy-Efficient, and Money-Saving Workspace
Woodstock, New York: Ceres Press, 1989. $17.95, available at bookstores, or from:
Ceres Press
P.O. Box 87, Woodstock, NY 12498
(914) 679-5573
This book offers complete information on designing an energy-efficient kitchen and helps you avoid costly mistakes.

Synergy available from:
P.O. Box 1854, Cathedral Station, New York, NY 10025
(212) 865-9595
A biannual sourcebook on nonpolluting energy sources, energy conservation, conferences, manufacturers, and more; $18 per year.

GARDENING

Organic gardening fact sheets available from:
Eco-Home Network
4344 Russell Ave., Los Angeles, CA 90027
(213) 662-5207
For $3 send for a packet of information on organic gardening, with fact sheets on composting and how to turn your yard into an instant garden using sheet mulching. If you visit LA, do make arrangements to visit the Eco-Home organic garden for inspiration.

Gray Water Use in the Landscape, by Robert Kourik
Edible Publications: Santa Rosa, 1988. $6, available from:
Edible Publications
P.O. Box 1841, Santa Rosa, CA 95402
(707) 874-2606

Let It Rot, by Stu Campbell
Pawnal, Vermont: Garden Way, 1975. $5.95, available at bookstores, or from:
Garden Way Publications
c/o Storey Communications
Schoolhouse Rd., Pawnal, VT 05261
(802) 823-5811

Armstrong's The Home and Garden Place
11321 W. Pico Blvd., West Los Angeles, CA 90064
(213) 477-8023
This book tells you everything you wanted to know about what goes into compost and how to make it, and includes bin designs.

Organically Grown Food, by Theodore Wood Carlat
Los Angeles: Wood Publishing, 1989. $4.50, available at bookstores, or from:

8833 W. Sunset Blvd. #304, Los Angeles, CA 90069
Packed with information, this slim paperback discusses organic and biodynamically grown foods, tells how to find and grow them, and lists manufacturers, distributors, and retailers that sell them.

Rodale's Garden Insect, Disease and Weed Identification Guide, by Miranda Smith and Anna Carr
Emmaus: Rodale Press, 1988. $21.95 hardcover, $15.95 softcover, available at bookstores, or from:
Rodale Books
33 E. Minor St., Emmaus, PA 18098
(800) 221-7945, (215) 967-5171
Learn how to tell good bugs from bad bugs, and how to keep pests in check safely and naturally. There are color photos and lots of drawings.

Rodale's Garden Problem Solver, by Jeff Ball
Emmaus: Rodale Press, 1990. $21.95, available at bookstores, or from:
Rodale Books
33 E. Minor St., Emmaus, PA 18098
(800) 221-7945, (215) 967-5171
This hardcover book describes problems you may have with various vegetables, fruits, berries, and herbs, and what to do about them. It includes sections on pests and diseases as well as on how to improve soil and about fertilizers and types of watering systems.

OREGON TILTH PUBLICATIONS:
Available from:
P.O. Box 218, Tualatin, OR 97062
692-4877

The Fifth Peace Seeds Research Journal, 1989-1990, by Alan Kapular Ph.D.
Tualatin: Oregon Tilth, 1990. $10 (from address above, add $1.50 postage and handling).
Research papers on species conservation and the new basis for complete nutrition.

Gardening Naturally, by Barbra Allen
Tualatin: Oregon Tilth, 1990. $6 (from address above, add $1.50 postage and handling).

For the home gardener who wants to avoid chemicals, here's a concise guide. It shows you how to build an ecologically balanced and healthy environment and includes plant lists especially for gardeners in the Pacific Northwest.

Oregon's Organic Law
Tualatin: Oregon Tilth, 1990. $1.
A copy of SB400 is available to Tilth members and nonmembers for $1. This law will explain what you get when you buy organic produce and the fines for mislabeling.

The Peace Papers, by Alan Kapuler Ph.D.
Tualatin: Oregon Tilth, 1990. $3 to $7 apiece.
Nutritional and genetic research on coevolutionary gardening is discussed in scientifically accurate terms. Ask for the list of available papers.

Standards and Guidelines for Growing and Processing Organic Foods (fourth edition)
Tualatin: Oregon Tilth, 1991. $5 members; $10 nonmembers.

The Transition Document, by Harry MacCormack and Alan Kapuler Ph.D.
Tualatin: Oregon Tilth, 1981. $10 (from address above, add $2.50 postage and handling).
In easy-to-understand form, here is all you need to know about the toxic environment, procedures for cleaning it, and the scientific basis for a vision beyond organic agriculture.

ISSUES AND GROUPS

Buzzworm: The Environmental Journal
Available from:
1818 Sixteenth St., Boulder, CO 80302
(303) 442-1969
A bimonthly magazine, *Buzzworm* has wonderful photos and articles on environmental issues. It's available in many bookstores and magazine stands; $18 per year.

Diet for a New America, by John Robbins
Walpole, New Hampshire: Stillpoint Publishing, 1987. $12.95, available at bookstores, or from:

Stillpoint Publishing
Walpole, NH 03608
(603) 756-9281
Yes, this book is about the environment, because eating animal products uses extra resources and contributes to pollution. This book may help you reduce your consumption of animal products, which would be a big help to the health of our planet.

Directory of Environmental Organizations
Available from:
Educational Communications
P.O. Box 35473, Los Angeles, CA 90035
(213) 559-9160
About four thousand names and addresses of environmental organizations; $32, or $200 for labels or diskettes.

E: The Environmental Magazine
Available from:
P.O. Box 6667, Syracuse, NY 13217-7934
(800) 825-0061
A clearinghouse of environmental information that lets you know what you can do to help; $20 per year.

50 Simple Things You Can Do to Save the Earth, by The EarthWorks Group
Berkeley: The EarthWorks Group, 1989. $4.95, available at bookstores, or from:
EarthWorks Press
Box 25, 1400 Shattuck Ave., Berkeley, CA 94709
(415) 841-5866
Primers should be easy to read, easy to follow, and not overwhelming—like this one. It deserves a place in everyone's home.

Garbage: The Practical Journal for the Environment
Available from:
P.O. Box 51647, Boulder, CO 80321-1647
(800) 274-9909
Our favorite environmental magazine, one of the very best, has clear, in-depth articles not found in others. It's practical, with a sense of humor; bimonthly, $21 per year.

The Green Consumer, by John Elkington, Julia Hailes, and Joel Makower
New York: Penguin Books, 1988. $8.95, available at bookstores
Here's a guide to easy life-style changes and products that won't harm the earth.

How to Make the World a Better Place: A Guide to Doing Good, by Jeffrey Hollender
New York: William Morrow, 1990. $9.95, available at bookstores
This fine book cites more than a hundred easy actions toward positive social changes.

P3: The Earth Based Magazine for Kids
Available from:
P.O. Box 52, Montgomery, VT 05470
(802) 326-4669
P3 is Planet Earth, the third planet from the sun, and the magazine named for it shows six- to twelve-year-olds how to take action. For example, it encourages letter-writing on environmental issues. It's published by a nonprofit organization of scientists, lawyers, teachers, environmentalists, and students; $14 per year (ten issues).

Reweaving the World, The Emergence of Ecofeminism, edited by Irene Diamond and Gloria Feman Orenstein
San Francisco: Sierra Club Books, 1990. $14.95, available at bookstores, or from:
Sierra Club Books
730 Polk St., San Francisco, CA 94109
(415) 923-5600
All the essays in this anthology are on ecofeminism, an environmental movement that encompasses a consciousness of the interconnectedness of all life, political action, and an earth-based spirituality. Included are essays by Julia Russell, founder of Eco-Home, and Riane Eisler, author of *The Chalice and the Blade—Our History, Our Future.*

Save Our Planet: 750 Everyday Ways You Can Help Clean Up the Earth, by Diane MacEachern
New York: Dell Publishing, 1988. $9.95, available at bookstores
Practical information on changes you can make in your home—some using the products cited in this directory and some you can make just by reminding yourself.

LIFE STYLE

Voluntary Simplicity: Toward a Way of Life That Is Outwardly Simple, Inwardly Rich, by Duane Elgin
William Morrow: New York, 1981. $7.95, available at bookstores, or from:
William Morrow and Co.
New York, NY 10016
(212) 889-3050
Live in balance with the environment by identifying less with material possessions and relating compassionately to friends, family, and neighbors. If you feel uncomfortable in the rat race and want to connect with the human race, this book can help you make some changes.

POLITICAL RESOURCES

The Almanac of American Politics: 1990, by Michael Barone; edited by Grant Ujifusa
Washington D.C.: National Journal Inc., 1989. $44.95, available from:
Macmillan Publishing Co.
866 Third Ave., New York, NY 10022
(800) 257-5755, (212) 702-2000
Information for groups organizing on a federal level.

The Corporate Address Book, by Michael Levine
New York: Perigee, 1990. $8.95, available at bookstores, or from:
Perigee, division of G.P. Putnam
200 Madison Ave., New York, NY 10016
(800) 631-8571, (212) 951-8400
This yearly periodical lists the addresses of companies and their subsidiaries so you can organize a letter-writing campaign.

National Boycott Newsletter
6506 Twenty-eighth Ave., Seattle, WA 98115
(206) 523-0421
This quarterly newsletter lists the reasons for and status of a number of current product boycotts, from food to cars; $5 per year.

Publications Catalog
New York: League of Women Voters, 1990. Free, available from:

League of Women Voters of the United States
1730 M St. N.W., Washington, D.C. 20036
(202) 429-1965
The league's free catalog lists low-cost books and booklets that explain how to be politically active in local and national issues.

USA Directory
Sacramento: Dutra Communications, 1990. $7, available from:
Dutra Communications
P.O. Box 1863, Sacramento, CA 95812
(916) 447-7773
Information on whom to contact and where on the federal level.

RECYCLING

Complete Trash: The Best Way to Get Rid of Practically Everything Around the House, by Norm Crampton
New York: M. Evans and Co., 1989. $10.20, available at bookstores, or from:
M. Evans and Co.
216 E. Forty-ninth St., New York, NY 10017
(212) 688-2810
When tomorrow's solutions feel overwhelming today, this book tells you where to begin.

Mr. Rumples Recycles, by Barbara Anne Coltharpe
Hyacinth House: Baton Rouge, 1989. $5.25, available at bookstore, or from:
Hyacinth House Publishers
P.O. Box 14603, Baton Rouge, LA 70898
(504) 767-6717
A twenty-five-page book on recycling and composting for children grades kindergarten through sixth.

"Reduce, Reuse, Recycle" (column), by Jeanne Roy
FOODday section of the Tuesday *Oregonian*

Resource Recycling
Available from:
P.O. Box 10540, Portland, OR 97210
227-1319

This monthly tells you more than you ever wanted to know about recycling around the country. With details of working programs in other cities, it's excellent for anyone who wants to go into a waste-management business, large or small. A subscription costs $42 per year.

SAFE-PRODUCTS CATALOGS

EcoSource Catalog
9051 Mill Station Rd., Bldg. E, Sebastopol, CA 95472
(800) 688-8345

Formerly Environmental Concerns, EcoSource offers a wide selection of environmental goods, from string bags and organic flea powder to compost and T-shirts. Printed on 100 percent recycled paper with soybean ink, almost every page has facts and figures. The research department tests all products for environmental soundness.

The Environmental Catalog
116 Fourth St., Santa Rosa, CA 95401
(800) 832-1986, (707) 542-1900
Fax (707) 542-4358

For fourteen years this company, Solar Energy, has worked to provide alternative energy options, especially in the form of electric vehicles and solar energy. Its catalog offers paper products, water saving devices, and even organic insecticides. Do you need biodegradable antifreeze or a motion-sensitive solar powered house light? You can find it here. All products carry a thirty-day full-refund guarantee.

Real Goods Catalog
966 Mazzoni St., Ukiah, CA 95482
(800) 762-7325

Real Goods carries the largest and most thorough selection of alternative energy products in the world, including irrigation systems, power-generating devices and systems, and composting toilets. From the complex to the very simple, it has items you will definitely want—like a solar AM radio for $11.

Seventh Generation Catalog
Colchester, VT 05446-1672
(800) 456-1177

The products offered include a wide range of recycled paper products plus water savers, recycling equipment, biodegradable cleaners, organic baby food, diapers, and much more. Everything has a money-back guarantee.

Walnut Acres Natural Foods Catalog
Penns Creek, PA 17862
(800) 433-3998

Here find certified organic food from soup to nuts, including grains, cereals, juices, vegetables, and meats. In fact, you can mail order everything you need for a healthy diet except fresh fruit and vegetables. The catalog even has juicers, pots and pans, and yogurt and yogurt cheese makers, for a completely stocked kitchen.

SAFE-PRODUCTS GUIDES

Clean and Green, by Annie Berthold Bond
Woodstock: Ceres Press, 1990. $6.45, available at bookstores, and from:
Ceres Press
P.O. Box 87, Woodstock, NY 12498
(914) 679-5573

The Earthwise Consumer, by Debra Lynn Dadd
Available from:
P.O. Box 1506, Mill Valley, CA 94942
(415) 383-5892

For $20 per year you get eight issues of information on products that are safe for you and the environment. Instead of going nuts trying to sort through new products, let Debra do it for you with up-to-the-minute recommendations.

Guide to Hazardous Products Around the Home (second edition)
Springfield, Missouri: Household Hazardous Waste Project, 1989. $8, available from:
Household Hazardous Waste Project
901 S. National St., Box 108, Springfield, MO 65804
(417) 836-5777

What do you have at home that's toxic? This tells you and gives safer alternatives.

Making the Switch: Alternatives to Using Toxic Chemicals in the Home
Sacramento: Golden Empire Health Planning Center, 1989. $1, available from:

Golden Empire Health Planning Center
P.O. Box 162997, Sacramento, CA 95816
A forty-page booklet on household toxic materials tells what you can make or buy that's safe for you and the environment.

Nontoxic and Natural: A Guide for Consumers: How to Avoid Dangerous Everyday Products and Buy or Make Safe Ones, by Debra Lynn Dadd
Los Angeles: J. P. Tarcher, 1986. $9.95, available at bookstores, or from:
J. P. Tarcher
5858 Wilshire Blvd., Los Angeles, CA 90036
(213) 935-9980
This book is a classic consumer guide to more than twelve hundred brand-name items rated for nontoxicity, five hundred mail-order sources, and four hundred formulas for everyday products you can easily make at home.

The Nontoxic Home: Protecting Yourself and Your Family from Everyday Toxins and Health Hazards, by Debra Lynn Dadd
Los Angeles: J. P. Tarcher, 1986. $9.95, available at bookstores, or from:
J. P. Tarcher
5858 Wilshire Blvd., Los Angeles, CA 90036
(213) 935-9980
Here's a comprehensive book on safe, natural alternatives to common hazardous household and personal care products, appliances, and office products.

SOCIALLY RESPONSIBLE INVESTMENTS

Catalyst
64 Main St., Montpelier, VT 05602
(802) 223-7943
Catalyst is a quarterly newsletter about socially responsible investment opportunities: sample, $7.50; one year, $25.

Clean Yield Publications
P.O. Box 1880, Greensboro Bend, VT 05842
(802) 533-7178
Clean Yield offers a monthly market newsletter with special supplements: $85 a year; trial issue, $3.

Economics as If the Earth Really Mattered, by Susan Meeker-Lowry
Santa Cruz: New Society Publishers, 1989. $9.95, available at bookstores, or from:
New Society Publishers
P.O. Box 582, Santa Cruz, CA 95061-0582
(800) 333-9093
A guide to socially conscious investing.

Green Review
Available from:
24861 Alicia Pkwy., Ste. C-293, Laguna Hills, CA 92653
(800) 825-7746
SRI Advisors publishes this monthly environmental investment newsletter: sample, $5; one year, $48.

In Business: The Magazine for Environmental Entrepreneuring
Available from:
Box 323, Emmaus, PA 18049
(215) 967-4136
Complete with a directory of environmental entrepreneurs throughout the country, this bimonthly magazine can help you turn your interest in the environment into a business that can help keep it—and you—green: $3.50 per issue or $21 per year, with a money-back guarantee.

Shopping for a Better World: A Quick and Easy Guide to Socially Responsible Supermarket Shopping
New York: Ballantine Books, 1989. $4.95, available at bookstores, or from:
Council on Economic Priorities
30 Irving Pl., New York, NY 10003
(212) 420-1133
In a series of charts, data on companies and products that are environmentally sound.

PUBLIC TRANSPORTATION

In Oregon local and state governments have worked together to provide forms of public transit in every county and urban area. This listing provides the major carriers. In larger population areas check between the white and yellow sections of your phone book for an information section that lists transit maps and phone numbers.

WILLAMETTE VALLEY
Albany Transit System and Linn-Benton Loop Bus
Information for both systems:
967-4318
Albany City Hall
250 Broadalbin St., P.O. Box 490, Albany, OR 97321
Albany Transit Times of Service: Monday to Friday 7 A.M. to 5:30 P.M. No service on holidays. Linn-Benton Loop Bus Times of Service: Monday to Friday 6:20 A.M. to 6:30 P.M. No service on holidays.

Cities and Sites Served: The Albany Transit System serves Albany proper. The Linn-Benton Loop Bus stops at: Albany, Corvallis, Hewlett-Packard, Linn-Benton Community College, and Oregon State College.

Columbia County Transit (COLCO)
Information:
397-4341
P.O. Box 141, St. Helens, OR 97501
Times of Service: Monday to Friday 7:30 A.M. to 5 P.M. No service on holidays.

City Served: St. Helens proper.
On Call: Clatskanie, Rainier, Scappose, Vernonia.

Corvallis Transit System
Information:
757-6998
P.O. Box 1083, Corvallis, OR 97338-1083
Times of Service: Monday to Friday 6:30 A.M. to 6:30 P.M. Saturday: 10 A.M. to 4:30 P.M. No service on major holidays.

City Served: Corvallis proper.

Lane Transit District (LTD)
Information:
687-5555
10th Ave. & Willamette St., Eugene, Oregon 97401
Times of Service: Monday to Friday 5:45 A.M. to 10:45 P.M. Saturday: 6:45 A.M. to 8:45 P.M. Sunday: 7:45 A.M. to 6:45 P.M.

Cities Served: Coburg, Lowell, Elmira, McKenzie Bridge, Eugene, Pleasant Hill, Fall Creek, Veneta, and Junction City.

LIFT
Information:
Molalla: (800) 621-5438
Wilsonville: 656-2300
1401 Washington St., Oregon City, OR 97045
Times of Service: Monday to Friday 5:30 A.M. to 7:30 A.M.
Cities Served: Molalla LIFT connects to Tri-Met in Oregon City. Wilsonville connects to Tri-Met at northern Wilsonville.

Salem Area Mass Transit
Information:
588-2885
3140 Del Webb Ave. N.E., Salem, OR 97301
Times of Service: Monday to Friday: 6 A.M. to 7:15 P.M. Saturday: 7:45 A.M. to 6:45 P.M. No service on major holidays.
Cities Served: Keizer, Salem. Service includes six Park and Ride lots, and a midday shuttle between downtown Salem and the Capital Mall.

Tri-County Metropolitan Transportation District of Oregon (Tri-Met)
Information:
General: 233-3511
Twenty-four-hour Call-A-Bus (specific route information): 231-3199
MAX schedule: 22-TRAIN
Senior and disabled services: 238-4952
Hearing-impaired information service TDD equipped: 238-5811
Trip planning: 233-3511
Carpooling: CARPOOL
For information by mail:
Tri-Met Consumer Programs
4012 S.E. Seventeenth Ave., Portland, OR 97202
Times of Service: Daily 5 A.M. to 1 A.M.
Cities Served: Beaverton, Canby, Cedar Hills, Cornelius, Fairview, Forest Grove, Gladstone, Gresham, Hillsboro, Lake Oswego, Milwaukie, Oregon City, Portland, Sherwood, Tigard, Troutdale, Tualatin, Wilsonville
In the 1989-1990 service year Tri-Met, with its combination of buses, MAX rapid transit, park and ride stations, and varieties of customer service, was named the nation's best mass transit system. The newly approved Westside Lightrail will further improve Tri-Met's service.

Woodburn Transit System
Information:
982-5245
270 Montgomery St., Woodburn, OR 97071
Times of Service: Monday to Friday 9 A.M. to 5 P.M. Saturday: 10 A.M. to 5 P.M.
Cities Served: Woodburn Transit serves Woodburn and connects with Tri-Met for Portland.

YAMCO and LINK
Information for McMinnville and Lafayette:
472-0457
P.O. Box 621, McMinnville, OR 97128
Information for Dundee and Newberg:
538-7433
Chehalem Valley Sr. Citizen's Council
404 E. Third St., Newberg, OR 97132
YAMCO Times of Service: Monday to Friday 8 A.M. to 5 P.M. No service on holidays. LINK Times of Service: Monday to Friday 6 A.M. to 7:45 A.M.
Cities Served: Yamco serves Dundee, McMinnville, Newberg. Link connects YAMCO and Lafayette to Tri-Met and Portland.

SOUTHERN OREGON
Basin Transit Service
Information:
883-2877
Senior and handicapped services: 883-1558
Customer Information Center
1130 Adams St., Klamath Falls, OR 97601
Times of Service: Monday to Friday: 6 A.M. to 7:30 P.M. Saturday: 7 A.M. to 7:30 P.M. No service on holidays.
City Served: Klamath Falls and environs.

Rogue Valley Transportation District
Information:
779-BUSS
Senior and handicapped services: 664-6674, 779-6785
Customer Information Center
3200 Crater Lake Ave., Medford, OR 97504

Times of Service: Monday to Friday 5 A.M. to 7:30 P.M. Saturday: 8 A.M. to 6 P.M. No service on holidays.

Cities Served: Ashland, Central Point, Jacksonville, Medford, Phoenix, Talent, and White City.

EASTERN AND CENTRAL OREGON

Hood River County Transit
Information:
386-4202
1020 Wilson St., Hood River, OR 97031
Times of Service: Monday to Friday 8 A.M. to 5 P.M.
Cities Served: Cascade Locks, Hood River, Parkdale, and Odell.
County-wide wheelchair-accessible service is available for the general public; call the day before to schedule.

Ontario Transit Bus
Information:
889-7681, 889-7884
City Hall
444 S.W. Fourth Ave., Ontario, OR 97914
Times of Service: Monday to Friday 8 A.M. to 5 P.M. Reservations are recommended.
City Served: Ontario and the immediate area.

Transcentral
Information:
382-0800
1631 N.E. Second, Ste. A, Bend, OR 97202
Times of Service: Daily 7 A.M. to 10 P.M.
City Served: Bend and a three-mile radius beyond.

THE COAST

Astoria Transit System (TBR Co.)
Information:
325-3521
City Hall
1095 Duane St., Astoria, OR 97103
Times of Service: Monday to Friday 6:30 A.M. to 7 P.M. No service on holidays.
City Served: Astoria and the immediate area.

FACT
Information:
997-3000
P.O. Box 2145, Florence, OR 97439
Times of Service: Daily twenty-four hours on an on-call basis.
City Served: Florence and the immediate area.

Newport Area Transit (NAT)
Information:
265-8088
Naterlin Community Center, Rm. 5, Newport, OR 97365
Times of Service: Daily 7:30 A.M. to 6:30 P.M.
City Served: Newport and the immediate area.

RECHARGEABLE BATTERIES, see BATTERIES

RECYCLED PAPER, see PAPER, RECYCLED

RECYCLED PRODUCTS ON THE MARKET

We need to support the recycling industries by buying recycled products. The process isn't complete when we send our used materials to recycling centers. If we don't buy recycled products (and patronize businesses with in-house recycling programs; see under Recycling) we will continue to scramble for someone to take our magazines, plastic, and tires. Here is an alphabetical list of vendors of recycled materials that are made in Oregon. Frequently these products are cheaper than their virgin competitors.

BEER IN RECYCLED BOTTLES

Blitz Weinhard Co.
1133 W. Burnside St., Portland, OR 97209
222-4351

Blitz Weinhard collects and refills approximately 75 percent of its beer bottles. It is the most consistent user of recycled bottles in the Oregon market.

BUILDING MATERIALS

Many materials can be reused, including doors, windows, fireplaces, pipe fittings, fixtures and brass. Prices are generally 25 percent to 50 percent lower except for items considered antiques.

Hippo Hardware
201 S.E. Twelfth Ave., Portland, OR 97214
231-1444
Besides recycling building materials, Hippo Hardware hires the homeless whenever possible.

Rejuvenation House Parts
901 N. Skidmore St., Portland, OR 97217
249-2048
Contact Jim Kelly.

BUMPERS, PROTECTIVE

Protective bumpers, pads made from recycled tires, can be used on trucks, trailers, docks, and other equipment. The customized price ranges from $5 to $80—comparable to that for similar virgin products, but the recycled products last about five years, versus one year for the virgin product.

Fred Herman and Dean Madox
Box 2522, Eugene, OR 97402
(No phone)

Scientific Development, Inc.
175 S. Danebo St., Eugene, OR
686-9844

CONCRETE CHUNKS

Lone Star Northwest
3510 S.W. Bond St., Portland, OR 97201
231-8488
Recycled concrete mix can be used in 75 percent of all standard grades—except in high-strength, specialty, or technical specifications. The price is the same as for virgin concrete. Contact Mark Lesky.

The Wall
407 S.W. Eleventh Ave., Portland, OR 97205
288-7881

Chunks of sidewalk and driveway concrete mixed with mortar produce a 90 percent recycled material for constructing retaining walls and pavement, and for decorative uses. It costs an average of a third less than virgin materials. There is no charge for the recycled material, only for labor and hauling. Most customers are residential. Contact Gordon McCutcheon.

ENVIROTEK PRODUCTS

John Inskeep Environmental Learning Center (ELC)
Clackamas Community College
19600 S. Molalla Ave., Oregon City, OR 97045
656-0155
To leave message (800) 322-3326
Fax 656-0155

The Envirotek-brand products manufactured by ELC include park benches, picnic tables, sign bases, and interpretive signs. For wetlands and wildlife habitats Envirotek offers bridges, nature walks, and wildlife viewing blinds; it also carries home landscape products, low-maintenance nest boxes, and artificial wildlife habitats. All items are 100 percent recycled plastic and other materials.

FLOOR MATS

RB Rubber
904 E. Tenth Ave., McMinnville, OR 97208
472-4691

Mats made from 100 percent recycled buffing rubber are used on running tracks, roofs, and industrial walkways and in weight rooms, horse stalls, and horse trailers. Contact John Whitney or Jay Pratt.

FOUNDATION VENTS

Molded Container Corp.
8823 S.E. Thirteenth St., Portland, OR
233-8601
Mailing address:
P.O. Box 82126, Portland, OR 97282

Vents made from 100 percent recycled polyethylene are used in housing and mobile home construction, at prices comparable to those of virgin materials.

INSULATION, CELLULOSE

Made of almost 100 percent recycled paper and chemicals, cellulose insulation costs 20 percent less than fiberglass. It burns more quickly and at a much lower temperature than fiberglass and presents more of an insurance risk. The efficiency of the two is about the same, but cellulose is lighter and easier to install.

STATEWIDE
Fred Meyer, Inc.

Pay 'N Pak

MANUFACTURER:
Energy King
1435 S.E. Ninety-eighth Ct., Clackamas, OR 97015
654-2655

LOGS, COMPRESSED WOOD

The logs we recommend are 100 percent recycled hardwood with no Douglas fir or pine and no petroleum binders. The wood used by Green Fields, Inc. is throwaway debris from furniture manufacturers.

STATEWIDE
Cub Foods and Waremart

Fred Meyer, Inc. (selected stores)

Larry's Sport Centers

WILLAMETTE VALLEY
Andy and Bax
324 S.E. Grand Ave., Portland, OR 97214
234-7538

THE COAST
Arch Cape Grocery
Hwy. 101, Arch Cape, OR 97102
436-2912

Parkview Grocery
12232 N.E. Beverly Dr., Newport, OR 97365
265-9822

MANUFACTURER:
Green Fields, Inc.
30770 Buck Heaven Rd., Hillsboro, OR 97123
628-2435
Contact Anita Grunsven.

OIL, REREFINED LUBRICATING

Lubricating oil has many industrial and automotive uses; in Oregon the rerefined products are limited to use as hydraulic oils and bar/chain lubricant. Rerefiners are unable to fully meet the demand for rerefined base oil because they cannot obtain enough used oil. Top quality rerefined oil is almost indistinguishable from others except with highly technical testing.

Fuel Processors, Inc.
4150 N. Suttle Rd., Portland, OR 97217
286-8352
Refines a small quantity of oil for small individual users, such as farmers and mechanics. Contact Bill Briggs.

PAPER BAGS FOR GROCERIES
STATEWIDE
Lamb's Market

Ray's Century

Thriftway

MANUFACTURER:
Willamette Industries, Inc.
5800 S.W. Western Ave., Beaverton, OR 97005
641-4455
Willamette Industries' Will-Cycle grocery bags are made with at least 40 percent previously used wood fibers. The company's four paper mills annually recycle 1.1 billion pounds of used corrugated boxes. For information, contact Doug Leland.

SEWAGE SLUDGE

Sewage sludge from the city of Portland is combined with sawdust and with bark, perlite, or both, for use as a soil amendment and component of potting mixes. It is not recommended for food crop production. Buy it in bulk (as it's sold primarily to landscapers) or in bags under the name "Garden Care" as a potting mix.

Dennis' 7 Dees Nursery and Landscaping
6025 S.E. Powell Blvd., Portland, OR 97206
771-1421
Contact Jan Bullock.

Gro-Land Garden Center
22566 S.E. Stark St., Gresham, OR 97030
665-7271
Contact Bernice Gadbaugh.

Milwaukie Floral Company
3306 S.E. Lake Rd., Milwaukie, OR 97222
659-7271
Contact Virginia Welderman.

North American Soils Inc.
5303 N. Columbia Blvd., Portland, OR 97203
285-5125
Contact Steve Lokey.

Oregon Fuel Company
570 N. Columbia Blvd., Portland, OR 97211
285-3674
Contact Carol Lukeroth.

SPEED BUMPS

Made of 99 percent recycled rubber from aircraft and truck tires, these bumps are more flexible, portable and gentle to your vehicle than others.

Fred Herman and Dean Madox
Box 2522, Eugene, OR 97402
(No phone)

Scientific Development, Inc.
175 S. Danebo St., Eugene, OR 97401
686-9844

STAINED GLASS

Bullseye Glass Co.
3722 S.E. Twenty-first Ave., Portland, OR 97213
232-8887
The recycled-glass content of stained glass from Bullseye varies but averages about 10 percent. Open to the general public, this firm is believed to be the only one in the industry selling recycled stained glass. Contact Norm Henry.

TOPSOIL

Portland Sand and Gravel
10717 S.E. Division St., Portland, OR 97266
252-3495
The Portland company sells 100 percent recycled material from area construction sites. This topsoil is about $1 per yard cheaper than from other sources. It is available to both landscape contractors and homeowners, during the summer.

RECYCLING

In 1971 Oregon recycling began in earnest with the passage of the nation's first Bottle Bill. Over the past two decades eighteen other programs have been developed to further encourage recycling. Today 90 percent of the state's residents participate in at least one recycling program, and more than half a million tons of material, or 20 percent of the state's municipal solid waste, is diverted from landfills each year.

The Recycling Opportunity Act of 1983 extended convenient curbside recycling to all households in cities with populations over four thousand, and established drop-off depots at all disposal sites in rural areas. Oregonians can easily recycle separated glass, newspaper, cardboard, tin, aluminum, and motor oil (as well as some plastics and yard debris in certain areas). There are special recycling programs for oil, lead-acid batteries, and used tires. Tax credit programs add incentives for recycling and for the creation of new products from recycled materials.

BATTERIES

Each year Oregonians discard six-hundred thousand lead-acid batteries. Eighty percent is recycled, but the remaining 20 percent accounts for much of the toxic lead found in landfills and solid-waste incinerator ash.

The 1989 Oregon legislature, in passing HB 3305, required retailers to take back used batteries for recycling. Penalties for improper disposal of lead-acid batteries include fines up to $500. During the first three years of the act any person may return one battery over the quantity purchased, and during that period one used lead-acid battery may be returned at a time even if a new one was not purchased.

All household batteries also should be recycled with hazardous wastes. The following two companies can help.

Environmental Pacific Corp.
16643 S.E. Roosevelt St., Lake Oswego, OR 97035
636-5779
Environmental Pacific charges $.50 per pound for the household batteries it recycles.

Starkey Custom Hearing Aids
Starkey Laboratories Northwest
2255 N.E. 194th, Portland, OR 97230
661-7424
Nationally Starkey's encourages the use of its zinc-air hearing aid batteries, which use only a trace of mercury. It will recycle any hearing aid batteries returned to a Starkey distributor (the distributor receives credit for them). Starkey sells these batteries to overseas recyclers and uses the income to fund hearing aids for people on limited incomes. Call for the distributor nearest you.

CONTACT PEOPLE

Your local garbage handlers can answer most questions you have about recycling; what they can't, ask the people listed here, by county. They can give you information concerning materials that can be recycled and locations of appropriate depots.

BAKER COUNTY
Loren Henry
Baker Sanitary Service

3048 Campbell St., Baker, OR 97814
523-2626

BENTON-LINN COUNTY
Jeff Andrews
Albany-Lebanon Sanitary
1214 S. Montgomery St., Albany, OR 97321
928-2551

Jeff Andrews
Corvallis Disposal Co.
P.O. Box 1, Corvallis, OR 97330
645-0444

Sherman Weld
Sweet Home Sanitation Service
P.O. Box 96, Sweet Home, OR 97386
367-3535

CLACKAMAS COUNTY
Metropolitan Service District
Recycling Information Office
2000 S.W. First Ave., Portland, OR 97201
224-5555

Susan Zioko
902 Abernethy Rd., Oregon City, OR 97405
655-8521

CLATSOP COUNTY
David Sypher
City of Astoria
1095 Duane St., Astoria, OR 97103
325-5821

Doug Thompson
Recycle NOW, Inc.
10 Sixth St. #207, Astoria, OR 97103
325-1230

Pete Anderson
Seaside Sanitary Service
734 Oceanway, Seaside, OR 97138
738-5717

COLUMBIA COUNTY
Glenn Higgins
Columbia County Land Development Service
Courthouse, St. Helens, OR 97051
397-1501

COOS COUNTY
Randy Anderson
Star of Hope Recycling
1712 Sheridan St., North Bend, OR 97459
756-1141

CROOK COUNTY
Gary Goodman
Prineville Disposal
P.O. Box J, Prineville, OR 97754
447-5208

CURRY COUNTY
Pete Smart, T. V. Skinner
Brookings Energy Facility, Inc.
P.O. Box 1240, Brookings, OR 97415
469-2425

DESHUTES COUNTY
Suzanne Johannsen
Bend Recycling Team
P.O. Box 849, Bend, OR 97709
388-3638

DOUGLAS COUNTY
Douglas John
Roseburg Disposal Co.
835 S.E. Sheridan St., Roseburg, OR 97470
673-7122

GILLIAM COUNTY
The Honorable Laura Pryor
Gilliam County Court
P.O. Box 427, Condon, OR 97823
384-6351

GRANT COUNTY
Barbara Miller-Sohr
Grant County Recycling
P.O. Box 622, John Day, OR 97845
575-0187

HARNEY COUNTY
Bob Christensen
P.O. Box 1106, Burns, OR 97720
573-6441

HOOD RIVER COUNTY
John Rath
Hood River Garbage Service
P.O. Box 757, Hood River, OR 97031
386-2272

JACKSON COUNTY
Bob Wenker, Lois Wenker, Gary Rigotti
Ashland Sanitary Service
170 Oak St., Ashland, OR 97520
482-1471

Dick Bottjer
Rogue Disposal Service
135 W. Main St., Medford, OR 97501
779-4161

JEFFERSON COUNTY
Don Wood
Jefferson County Road Dept.
P.O. Box 709, Madras, OR 97741
475-3627

JOSEPHINE COUNTY
Pat Fahey
Southern Oregon Sanitation
P.O. Box 6000, Grants Pass, OR 97527

Bob Hutsell
SPARC
P.O. Box 1406, Grants Pass, OR 97526
476-8241

KLAMATH COUNTY
Cheryl Kenney
2348 Orchard Ave., Klamath Falls, OR 97601
883-2781

LAKE COUNTY
Jeremiah O'Leary
Lake County Commissioner
513 Center St., Lakeview, OR 97630
947-6004

LANE COUNTY
Mike Hamblin
BRING Recycling
P.O. Box 885, Eugene, OR 97440
683-3637

LINCOLN COUNTY
Mary Arman
P.O. Box 511, Depoe Bay, OR 97341
765-2575

MALHEUR COUNTY
Scott Wilson
Ontario Sanitary Service
1208 S.E. Sixth St., Ontario, OR 97914
889-5719

MARION COUNTY
Mary Kanz
Mid-Valley Garbage and Recycling Assoc.

3680 Brooklake Rd. N.E., Salem, OR 97305
390-1370

MORROW COUNTY
Don Ball
Morrow County Public Works Dept.
P.O. Box 453, Lexington, OR 97839
676-9061 x17

MULTNOMAH COUNTY
Metropolitan Service District
Recycling Information Office
2000 S.W. First Ave., Portland, OR 97201
224-5555

Bruce Walker
Solid Waste Division
Bureau of Environmental Services
City of Portland
1120 S.W. Fifth Ave., Portland, OR 97204
796-7772

POLK COUNTY
Steve Briles
Dallas Garbage Disposal
1030 W. Ellendale St., Dallas, OR 97338
623-2552

SHERMAN COUNTY
Glen Pierce
Wasco-Sherman Public Health Dept.
400 E. Fifth St., The Dalles, OR 97058
296-4636

TILLAMOOK COUNTY
Jon Oshel, Director
Tillamook County Department of Public Works
503 Marlof Loop Rd., Tillamook, OR 97141
842-3419

UMATILLA COUNTY
Mike Jewett
Sanitary Disposal, Inc.
P.O. Box 316, Hermiston, OR 97838
567-8842

Roger Emery
Horizon Enterprises
608 N. Russell St., Milton-Freewater, OR 97862
938-5650

Sue McHenry
Pendleton Sanitary Service
P.O. Box 1405, Pendleton, OR 97801
276-1271

UNION COUNTY
Ron Larvik
City Garbage Service
1202 Willow St., La Grande, OR 97850
963-5459

WALLOWA COUNTY
The Honorable Patricia Combes
Wallowa County
101 S. River St., Enterprise, OR 97828
426-3586

WASCO COUNTY
Art Braun
The Dalles Disposal
1134 Oak Dr., The Dalles, OR 97058
289-5149

WASHINGTON COUNTY
Metropolitan Service District
Recycling Information Office
2000 S.W. First Ave., Portland, OR 97201
224-5555

Joan Grimm
Department of Health and Human Services
Washington County
155 N. First Ave., Hillsboro, OR 97124
648-8722

WHEELER COUNTY
The Honorable Marilyn Garcia
Wheeler County Court
P.O. Box 327, Fossil, OR 97830
763-2911

YAMHILL COUNTY
Judy Toliver, Bob Emrick
City Sanitary
P.O. Box 509, McMinnville, OR 97138
472-3176

Marvin Schneider
Newberg Garbage Service
P.O. Box 990, Newberg, OR 97132
538-1388

Darol Funk
West County Sanitary Service
245 N.E. Hill St., Sheridan, OR 97378
843-3231

HAZARDOUS WASTE

Hazardous chemicals are used throughout the home and workshop: pesticides, most cleaners and polishes, oil, gasoline, antifreeze, and paints and paint-related products. The best approach to this waste problem is not to contribute to it. Find alternatives, but if you can't find alternatives, buy only what you need.

Read the label. These key words tell you if a product is dangerous: *poison, corrosive, caustic, volatile, flammable, explosive.*

If you toss hazardous waste in your trash, you'll endanger garbage haulers or workers at transfer stations and landfills, and contribute to soil and groundwater contamination. If you dump these wastes down your drain, you'll contribute to toxic overloading at sewage treatment plants or in your septic system. If you dump them in a ditch, storm drain, or your backyard, they'll find their way into soil, groundwater, and the surface water of lakes and streams.

To learn how to dispose of hazardous waste properly, call the Department of Environmental Quality (DEQ) at (800) 452-4011; or if you live in the tri-county area contact the Metro Recycling Information Center at 224-5555. Your county office of the State Health Division and your local fire department can also provide explanations.

You might be able to recycle hazardous products; for example, paints, hobby supplies, and pesticides could be useful to neighbors, friends, theater groups, church groups, schools, garden clubs, or the Extension Service.

If you become exposed to any hazardous substance, contact the Poison Control Center, (800) 452-7165.

PAPER PRODUCTS, GLASS, METAL, OIL, AND PLASTIC

Curbside recycling programs collect separated newspaper, cardboard, glass, tin, aluminum, and motor oil (in certain areas some plastics and yard debris are included), but this is not everything that can be recycled. The recyclers below accept a wider range of materials. Individuals and groups interested in fund raising can contact these companies for more information. The materials handled by recyclers in this section include:

- Corrugated cardboard and kraft paper bags
- High-grade papers, including ledger and computer paper
- Mixed paper (the lowest grade)
- Newspaper
- Container glass
- Aluminum
- Ferrous metal
- Nonferrous metals other than tinned steel cans, such as lead and zinc
- Tinned steel cans
- Used motor oil and hydraulic fluid
- Plastics
  Polyethylene, as from milk, juice, and water jugs
  Rigid-brittle polystyrene, such as cottage-cheese, sour-cream, and some yogurt containers; if a container cracks when squeezed it fits in this category
  Rigid-pliable plastics, such as margarine tubs, shampoo bottles,

some yogurt containers, and other assorted containers; if the container does not crack when squeezed, it fits here

Soft plastic, such as polyethylene films; plastic bags (including bread wrappers and trash bags) and Saran-brand and other plastic films

In the tri-county area (Multnomah, Washington, and Clackamas) recycling companies are too numerous to list here; to learn which are nearest you check the Yellow Pages under Recycling Services. For answers to recycling questions call the Metro Recycling Information Center at 224-5555, from 8:30 A.M. to 5 P.M. Monday through Friday. In the Eugene area (for which several recyclers are listed here) BRING Recycling answers questions: 683-3637.

WILLAMETTE VALLEY

Source Recycling: Albany
840 Thirtieth Ave. S.W., Albany, OR 97331
928-0623
Pays for: aluminum, corrugated cardboard and kraft paper bags, high-grade papers (including ledger and computer paper), newspaper, and tinned steel cans.
Accepts: container glass, and used motor oil and hydraulic fluid.
Contact Dean Moore.

Willamette Industries, Inc.
3251 Old Salem Rd. N.E., Albany, OR 97231
926-2281
Pays for: corrugated cardboard and kraft paper bags.

Eugene Mission
1542 W. First Ave., Eugene, OR 97440
344-3251
Pays for: newspaper, corrugated cardboard and kraft paper bags, and high-grade papers (including ledger and computer paper).
Accepts: mixed paper (the lowest grade).
Contact Ernie Unger.

NW Resource Recycling
1680 Irving Rd., Eugene, OR 97402
461-2000

Pays for: aluminum, container glass, corrugated cardboard and kraft paper bags, high-grade papers (including ledger and computer paper), ferrous metal, and tinned steel cans.
Accepts: used motor oil and hydraulic fluid.
Contact Jim Walpole.

Sessler Inc.—Eugene
111 Pacific Hwy. 99N, Eugene, OR 97402
686-0515
Pays for: aluminum, ferrous metal, and nonferrous metals other than tinned steel cans.
Contact Ray Sessler.

Weyerhauser
2070 Cross St., Eugene, OR 97402
688-2123
Pays for: aluminum, corrugated cardboard and kraft paper bags, and newspaper.
Accepts: container glass, mixed paper (the lowest grade), tinned steel cans, and used motor oil and hydraulic fluid.
Contact Pamela Burnett.

Cascade Steel Mills, Inc.
3200 N. Hwy. 99W, McMinnville, OR 97303
472-4181
Pays for: ferrous metal.

Smurfit Newsprint—Newburg
P.O. Box 70, Newburg, OR 97132
538-2151
Pays for: newspaper.
Contact Wayne Barlow.

Smurfit Newsprint—Philomath
351 N. Fifteenth St., Philomath, OR 97370
929-3215
Pays for: newspaper.

City Recycling
3570 Cherry Ave. N.E., Salem, OR 97303
390-0973

Pays for: aluminum, ferrous metal, and nonferrous metals other than tinned steel cans.

Clayton Ward Company
1620 Candlewood Dr. N.E., Salem, OR 97303
393-8700
Pays for: aluminum, container glass, corrugated cardboard and kraft paper bags, ferrous metal, newspaper, nonferrous metals other than tinned steel cans.
Accepts: mixed paper (the lowest grade), and used motor oil and hydraulic fluid.
Contact Bill Puntney.

Garten Foundation
1425 McGilchrist St. S.E., Salem, OR 97309
581-4473
Pays for: aluminum, container glass, corrugated cardboard and kraft paper bags, high-grade papers (including ledger and computer paper), newspaper, and nonferrous metals other than tinned steel cans.
Accepts: ferrous metal, tinned steel cans, and used motor oil and hydraulic fluid.
Contact John Matthews.

Western States Scrap Processing
3536 Belvedere St. N.W., Salem, OR 97304
378-7300
Pays for: aluminum, ferrous metal, and nonferrous metals other than tinned steel cans.
Accepts: tinned steel cans.
Contact John Graham or Jerry Graham.

Smurfit Newsprint—Sweet Home Division
1400 Eighteenth Ave.
P.O. Box 467, Sweet Home, OR 97386
367-6157
Pays for: newspaper.

SOUTHERN OREGON
Sessler Inc.—Grants Pass
605 Agness Ave., Grants Pass, OR 97526
479-4605

Pays for: aluminum, ferrous metal, and nonferrous metals other than tinned steel cans.
Contact John Meyer.

Sessler Inc.—Klamath Falls
2933 Hilyard Ave., Klamath Falls, OR 97603
882-5022
Pays for: aluminum, ferrous metal, and nonferrous metals other than tinned steel cans.
Accepts: tinned steel cans.
Contact Charles Kujawski.

Southern Oregon Recycling Center
640 Mason Way, Medford, OR 97501
779-8065
Pays for: aluminum, corrugated cardboard and kraft paper bags, ferrous metal, high-grade papers (including ledger and computer paper), newspaper, and nonferrous metals other than tinned steel cans.
Accepts: container glass, plastic, and tinned steel cans.
Contact Gene Kezer.

McGovern Metals
3801 Hwy. 995, Roseburg, OR 97470
679-7012
Pays for: aluminum, ferrous metal, and nonferrous metals other than tinned steel cans.
Accepts: tinned steel cans.
Contact Jim McGovern.

ABC Recycling
2645 Ave. G, White City, OR 97501
826-3335
Pays for: aluminum, corrugated cardboard and kraft paper bags, high-grade papers (including ledger and computer paper), and newspaper.
Accepts: container glass, and plastic.
Contact Ed Hurst.

Sessler Inc—White City
2625 Ave. G, White City, OR 97503

826-5788

Pays for: aluminum, ferrous metal, and nonferrous metals other than tinned steel cans.

Contact Fred Fisher.

EASTERN AND CENTRAL OREGON

Sessler Inc.—Bend
110 S.E. Fifth St., Bend, OR 97702
382-8471

Pays for: aluminum, ferrous metal, and non-ferrous metals other than tinned steel cans.

Contact Dan McCormick.

Sanitary Disposal, Inc.
P.O. Box 316, Hermiston, OR 97838
567-8842

Pays for: newspaper.

Accepts: aluminum, corrugated cardboard and kraft paper bags, ferrous metal, nonferrous metals other than tinned steel cans.

Contact Mike Jewett.

A & P Recycling
280 Webber Rd., The Dalles, OR 97058
296-3056

Pays for: aluminum, corrugated cardboard and kraft paper bags, high-grade papers (including ledger and computer paper), and newspaper.

Accepts: container glass, and plastic.

Contact Paul Lepinski.

THE COAST

International Paper Co.
P.O. Box 854, Gardiner, OR 97441
271-2151

Pays for: corrugated cardboard and kraft paper bags.

Contact Leo Naapi.

Weyerhauser—North Bend Mill
Jordan Point Rd., North Bend, OR 97459
756-5171

Pays for: corrugated cardboard and kraft paper bags.
Contact Connie Boddie.

Georgia Pacific Corporation
#1 Butler Bridge Rd., Toledo, OR 97391
336-2211
Pays for: corrugated cardboard and kraft paper bags.
Contact Bill Parsons, buyer, secondary fiber.

RECYCLING BY BUSINESSES IN-HOUSE

These Oregon businesses have innovative in-house recycling and environmental practices. Each time we buy a product or service from one of these companies we are encouraging other businesses to imitate their practices.

Blitz-Weinhard Brewing Co.
1133 W. Burnside St., Portland, OR 97209
222-4351
Blitz-Weinhard is one of the few breweries in the nation to recycle its glass bottles. Washing and refilling bottles requires much less energy than manufacturing new glass, and saves natural resources. Blitz also sells its own waste paper for reuse, returns all-aluminum cans to aluminum manufacturers, recovers heat generated in the brewing process, via heat exchangers, and sells spent yeast and grain for livestock feed locally.

First Interstate Bank of Oregon
1300 S.W. Fifth Ave., Portland, OR 97201
225-2111
First Interstate Bank has an environmental task force, a group that deals only with environmental issues. It encourages employees to assist with the in-house recycling program and to contribute environmental ideas. The bank primarily uses only white paper because it can be recycled through Wastech, a resource recovery firm. First Interstate is planning to expand its own use of recycled paper and prints its newsletter on recycled stock. It also makes its buildings as energy efficient as possible.

First Interstate holds an environmental fair to educate employees about environmental issues, and it offers a $15 monthly subsidy toward bus passes and Tri-Met one-way bus tickets.

Along with Friends of Trees and neighborhood associations, the bank sponsors an annual tree planting. This year one hundred trees will be planted in North Portland. A different neighborhood will benefit each year from the program.

Fred Meyer, Inc.
3800 S.E. Twenty-second Ave., Portland, OR 97242
232-8844

The environmental products on Fred Meyer's shelves are verified by a not-for-profit certification company before they are awarded the Green Cross Recycling Seal of Approval. Both the product and package must be made from at least 50 percent recycled materials. The manufacturer must have an aggressive solid-waste-reduction policy and also must meet a "no detected residue" standard for toxic emissions and effluents. These are tough tests; only fifty paper products and fire logs have passed.

Fred Meyer was the first major retailer in the Pacific Northwest to adopt a private pesticide-residue testing program for fruits and vegetables. All stores offer brochures on recycling and composting, and the grocery bags (Green Cross approved) are imprinted with recycling information. Fred Meyer stocks only phosphate-free detergents.

The company has received numerous state and national awards for its fifteen years of in-house recycling. In 1989 it recycled more than fifteen thousand tons. It conducts water and energy-conservation audits throughout its facilities, and looks for safer substitutes for the ozone-destroying chemicals in its air conditioning and refrigeration equipment.

Fred Meyer, Inc. encourages its manufacturers to eliminate unnecessary packaging wherever possible. It also does not buy its house-brand tuna from countries that support the use of driftnets.

Lawyer's Coalition
Dick Roy, Founder
244-0026

Thirty-five law firms in Portland, including ten of the largest in the state, have formed a recycling coalition. Each firm is represented by a lawyer and staff member. This group meets once every two months, and a seven-member steering committee meets once a month. These legal firms use boxes instead of wastepaper baskets, collecting office paper for recycling. They avoid yellow legal pads, and they insist that food services delivering their lunches use recycled paper bags and no Styrofoam. Some of the firms use letterhead on recycled paper.

The group is also urging The Oregon Bar Association not to print material on glossy paper, and has suggested that the courts use both paper sides for mimeographed material.

Tektronix
Howard Vollum Industrial Park, Beaverton, OR 97005
627-7111

Tektronix' recycling program brings in approximately $2.7 million a year. As an incentive, a large percentage of this is credited proportionally to the departments that supplied the recycled materials.

Instead of wastebaskets, boxes are positioned at desks and near printers and coffee machines, and discarded paper is collected, sorted, and then along with bailed cardboard is sold to Weyerhaeuser for recycling. For the two million pounds of paper collected last year Tektronix was paid $175,000, and 1.2 million pounds of used metal brought in $432,000.

Circuit boards, connectors, and other manufactured items are dismantled to recover precious metals, such as gold, silver, platinum, and palladium. Last year this earned Tektronix $1.7 million.

Consumers can call 627-6769 to find out about sales of the company's used desks and office furniture. Other companies and mills may purchase used process machinery from Tektronix.

TIRES

In 1987 Oregon established the Waste Tire Reimbursement Program to clean up the nearly two million tires discarded in the state each year. Funded by a $1 fee on all new tires sold, the program supplies incentives and reimbursement to companies that use waste tires, as well as providing money for cleanup of existing tire piles. For information call your nearest tire retailer, or contact the Department of Environmental Quality: state-wide, (800) 452-4011; in Portland, 229-5808.

YARD DEBRIS

You have to be a bit of a detective to make sure your yard debris does not end up in a landfill. Once you decide whether to haul it away yourself or to hire someone else for the job, call your county representatives listed under Recycling, Contact People. They can direct you to recycling centers (listed immediately below) or pickup and chipping services (also below) that turn brush into mulch.

There are proposals to include yard debris in curbside recycling. Since this debris accounts for 11 percent of landfill space and is easily turned into a reuseable product, we all need to support this change.

If you have a pickup truck and live in the Willamette Valley, you can take your yard and garden clippings to one of the following recycling centers for less than a landfill charges. (A standard-sized pickup truck load with the bed filled level holds about two and a half cubic yards.)

WILLAMETTE VALLEY

City of Beaverton
4950 S.W. Hall Blvd., Beaverton, OR 97005
644-4424
Charges $5 per cubic yard. This address is the old City Hall parking lot.

McFarlane's Bark, Inc.
13345 S.E. Johnson Rd., Clackamas, OR 97015
659-4240
Charges $4 per cubic yard ($2 minimum).

Unified Sewerage Agency
770 S. First Ave., Hillsboro, OR 97123
648-8716, 648-8622
Charges $5 per cubic yard ($5 minimum); no stumps, root balls, or sod. This address is the Hillsboro treatment plant.

American Container Service and Recycling
9707 N. Columbia Blvd., Portland, OR 97203
286-0886
Charges $7 per standard pickup load for leaves and grass; $9 per standard pickup load for branches, limbs, and woody waste.

Dees Debris
4485 S.E. Johnson Creek Blvd., Portland, OR 97222
771-9504
Accepts limbs and brush only; no grass or leaves. Call for updated information.

East County Recycling
12409 N.E. San Rafael St., Portland, OR 97230
253-0867
Charges $16.50 minimum fee for six hundred pounds or less. Any

amount over six hundred pounds is $55 per ton. Call for details about stumps.

St. Johns Landfill
9363 N. Columbia Blvd., Portland, OR 97203
286-9613
Charges $10 per load for a car or pickup. Other vehicles or trailers are charged $25 per ton.

Sunflower Recycling
2345 S.E. Gladstone St., Portland, OR 97202
238-1640
Charges $5 per cubic yard. Sunflower will take stumps narrower than one foot and branches shorter than six feet; no dirt, sod, or lumber.

Grimm's Fuel Company
18850 S.W. Cipole Rd., Tualatin, OR 97062
692-3756
Charges $4 per cubic yard; also accepts small scrap lumber and pallets.

Minsinger's Floral Nursery
655 S. Rosemont Rd., West Linn, OR 97068
636-1843
Drop off leaves, grass clippings, shavings, and stable manure, free; no brush, limbs, or woody waste.

West Linn Recycling Center
4001 Willamette Falls Dr., West Linn, OR 97068
656-4211
Charges $.50 per plastic bag or $3 to $6.50 per load, depending on size (West Linn residents only).

PICKUP AND CHIPPING SERVICES:

Many tree services haul your yard debris to a landfill. Environmental pickup and chipping services (those that use your brush to make bark dust or compost) are often seasonal, the service people work out of their homes, and they aren't listed in the phone book (they rely on classified ads and referrals through recycling centers). We have tracked down the phone numbers of some of these services in the Willamette Valley.

Contact these people to ask for their minimum fee. You might want to work with some neighbors and hire a chipper.

Beaver Bite Chipping
656-7805
Picks up leaves and grass only when you contract for chipping service. Serves west of the Willamette River.

Brownlee Chipper Service
254-5240
Picks up leaves and grass only when you contract for chipping service. Serves the Portland metropolitan area.

Chip Away
246-4695
Does stump grinding only. Serves the south side of Portland.

Chip-Rite
256-5877
Picks up leaves and grass with or without chipping service, and offers a senior discount. Serves the Portland metropolitan area.

Cloudburst Recycling
281-8075
Picks up grass, leaves, brush, and small tree trimmings; no stumps or sod. Service is limited to regular north, northeast, and southwest Portland customers, but drop boxes are available.

Dees Debris
771-9504
Picks up brush and limbs only. Serves the Portland metropolitan area.

George Esh
282-7188
Offers chipping service only. Serves the east side of Portland.

Lawrence Land Clearing Service
682-3653
Offers land clearing and stump grinding only. Chipped material is left

at your site; no hauling. Serves the West Hills, Lake Oswego, Milwaukie, and Oregon City.

Miller's Materials
245-3626
Picks up leaves and grass with or without chipping service. Serves west of the Willamette River.

Oregon City Garbage Company
656-8403
Weekly pickup is offered on the same day as garbage service. Small materials must be in plastic bags, boxes, or garbage cans, and branches must not be longer than four feet. Serves Oregon City and Gladstone.

Paul's Recycling
252-2711
Besides chipping will pick up lumber for a fee. Serves east Multnomah County.

Steve Bowerman
656-7234
Prefers jobs of at least 10 cubic yards and can handle up to 200 cubic yards. Serves the east side of Portland.

Sunflower Recycling
238-1640
In a limited area—Banfield Freeway to Powell Blvd. and Willamette River to Sixtieth Ave.—picks up vegetation, brush, and smaller branches and stumps. There is no pickup November 1 through March 31.

Trees by Joe
292-6309
Picks up leaves and grass only when you contract for chipping service.

RIDE SHARING, see PUBLIC TRANSPORTATION
SEEDS, ORGANIC
WILLAMETTE VALLEY
Vollstedt's Green Thumb
410 Pacific Blvd. S.W., Albany, OR 97321

928-2521
Sells Territorial seeds.

First Alternative
1007 S.E. Third St., Corvallis, OR 97333
753-3115
Sells Peace Seeds.

Down to Earth Farm and Garden
Fifth Ave. & Olive St., Eugene, OR 97402
342-6820
Sells Peace Seeds, Abundant Life, and Territorial.

Gray's Garden Shop
737 W. Sixth Ave., Eugene, OR 97402
345-1569
Both stores sell Territorial seeds.

444 E. Main St., Springfield, OR 97478
747-2301

Oregon Garden Store
333 S. State St., Lake Oswego, OR 97034
697-3635
Sells Shepherd's Garden seeds.

Dennis' 7 Dees
6025 S.E. Powell Blvd., Portland, OR 97206
777-1422
All three stores sell Abundant Life seeds.

10445 S.W. Barnes Rd., Portland, OR 97225
297-1058

1090 McVey Ave., Lake Oswego, OR 97034
636-4660

Drake's 7 Dees
16519 S.E. Stark St., Portland, OR 97233
255-9225
Sells Territorial seeds.

Earth Mercantile
6345 S.W. Capitol Hwy., Portland, OR 97201
246-4935
Sells Abundant Life seeds.

Nature's Fresh Northwest
5909 S.W. Corbett St., Portland, OR 97219
244-3934
All four stores sell Territorial seeds in season.

3449 N.E. Twenty-fourth Ave., Portland, OR 97212
288-3414

6344 S.W. Capitol Hwy., Portland, OR 97225
244-3110

4000 S.W. 117th Ave., Beaverton, OR 97005
646-3824

Northwest Garden Spot
2635 N.W. Thurman St., Portland, OR 97210
274-2439
Sells Territorial and Abundant Life seeds.

People's Food Store
3029 S.E. Twenty-first Ave., Portland, OR 97214
232-9051
Sells Abundant Life seeds.

Portland Nursery
5050 S.E. Stark St., Portland, OR 97215
231-5050
Sells Abundant Life seeds.

SOUTHERN OREGON

Chet's Garden Center
229 S.W. H St., Grants Pass, OR 97526
476-4424
Sells Territorial seeds.

Redwood Nursery
1290 Redwood Ave., Grants Pass, OR 97527
476-2642
Sells Southern Oregon Organic Seeds.

MAIL ORDER:
These companies sell organic or untreated, heirloom, or open-pollinated seeds, some of the best you'll find.

Abundant Life Seed Foundation
P.O. Box 772, Port Townsend, WA 98368
(206) 385-7192

Bountiful Gardens/Ecology Action
5798 Ridgewood Rd., Willits, CA 95490
(No phone)
Carries homegrown, untreated seeds.

Burrell Seed Growers Co.
P.O. Box 150, Rocky Fort, CO 81067
(303) 254-3318

Garden City Seeds
P.O. Box 297, Victor, MT 59875
(406) 961-4837

Johnny's Selected Seeds
Foss Hill Rd., Albion, ME 04910
(207) 437-9294
Carries mostly untreated seeds; some are homegrown.

Meadow Brook Herb Garden
Rt. 138, Wyoming, RI 02898
(401) 539-7603
Carries biodynamic herb seeds.

Nichols Garden Nursery
1190 N. Pacific Hwy., Albany, OR 97321
928-9280
Don't miss Nichols' once-a-year plant sale. Besides finding rare herbs and plants you can wander through the herb gardens.

Pacific Seeds
2385 S.E. Thompson St., Corvallis, OR 97333
752-0421

Peace Seeds
Alan Kapuler
2385 S.E. Thompson St., Corvallis, OR 97333
752-0421

Founder Alan Kapuler, who has a Ph.D. in molecular biology, realized seventeen years ago "it was no good to have beautiful laboratories if the beautiful diversity of living species vanished." Since then he has developed Peace Seeds, a wholesale seed outlet with 750 kinds of plant seeds organized by their biological kinship. He will send you a free list, or the more detailed catalog ($3.50). It takes 100 million years for a blooming plant to evolve, and Alan believes many of these plants only will survive through the efforts of the backyard gardner.

Alan Kapuler, John Sundquist, and Olafur Brentmar are designing a model gene-pool resource Coevolutionary Garden at River's Turn Farm. They welcome visitors there:

31139 Lane's Turn Road, Eugene, OR 97401.

Shepherd's Garden Seeds
6116 Hwy. 9, Felton, CA 95018
(408) 335-5400

Southern Oregon Organics
1130 Tetherow Rd., Williams, OR 97544

Organic heirloom seeds, open-pollinated and never treated with fungicides, are also all grown without animal by-products.

Territorial Seed Company
P.O. Box 157, Cottage, OR 97424
942-9547

Territorial seeds are grown with organic fertilizers and without chemical pesticides.

SEWAGE SLUDGE, see RECYCLED PRODUCTS

SHOPPING BAGS, see BAGS

Shower Heads, Low-Flow

In 1989 the new Oregon Plumbing Code required that all shower heads on the market deliver *fewer* than three gallons per minute (compared to a more typical six), and a Department of Energy study has determined that most models now being sold meet that limit. If you haven't replaced your old shower head with a new low-flow head, take a look at how much you could save.

Savings with a Low-flow Shower Head

TOTAL MINUTES OF DAILY SHOWERS	WATER SAVED ANNUALLY (IN GAL.)	COST OF WATER SAVED ANNUALLY (@$.70/100 CU. FT.*)	COST OF WATER HEATING SAVED ANNUALLY (@$.05/KWH*)
10	14,600	$13.62	$74.85
15	21,900	20.44	112.27
20	29,200	27.25	149.70
30	43,800	40.88	224.55

*This savings applies to houses on metered water systems that exceed any monthly minimum allowance. Water and energy costs are typical of Portland, Oregon in mid 1990.

When looking to a low-flow shower head for savings, don't forget your hot water heater. Set the thermostat at 120°, or at 140° if you have a dishwasher. Also, insulate your water heater; vinyl-covered fiberglass insulating jackets can be found at most hardware stores for about $10. These measures can save an additional $5 a month.

MAIL ORDER:
Co-op America
c/o Order Service
10 Farrell St., South Burlington, VT 05403
(800) 456-1177

The Europa shower head, in chrome and eleven colors, costs $12 (for chrome) to $19. There are lower prices on all items for Co-op America members.

Ecological Water Products
266 Main St., Ste. 18, Medfield, MA 02052
(800) 926-NOVA

The Nova B6401 (in chrome) costs $8.75 and uses 1.1 to 2.1 gallons per minute.

EcoSource
9051 Mill Station Rd., Bldg. E, Sebastopol, CA 95472
(800) 688-8345
A variety of showerheads cost from $9.95 to the highly touted Spa 2000 for $19.95.

Environmental Marketing Association
P.O. Box 70, Ojai, CA 93024
(805) 646-4647
If you want a full shower, try the Spa 2000 shower head. It loads the water with air and reduces flow from 6 gallons per minute to 2.5, saving you an estimated 11,400 gallons per person each year and hundreds of dollars in water heating costs; $19.95.

Real Goods
966 Mazzoni St., Ukiah, CA 95482
(800) 762-7325
The Nova B6401 (in chrome), which uses 1.1 to 2.1 gallons per minute, is $15.95.

Seventh Generation
Colchester, VT 05446-1672
(800) 456-1177
The Europa shower head in chrome and four colors is $13.95.

Solar Electric
116 Fourth St., Santa Rosa, CA 95401
(800) 832-1986, (707) 542-1900
Fax (707) 542-4358
Standard and "designer" shower heads cost $9.95 and $24.95. A water heater jacket is $11.95.

SOAKER HOSES, *see* WATER CONSERVATION PRODUCTS

*S*OIL AMENDMENTS, ORGANIC..

Pure yard waste such as grass, leaves, trimmings, and scrap lumber that is used as a mulch conserves moisture and reduces weeds. Organic fertilizers feed your plants, condition your soil, and put beneficial organisms and minerals in it. We list sources of these kinds of amendments, and more. (If you're not going to eat what you grow look into using sewage sludge, under Recycled Products on the Market.)

STATEWIDE

Many chain stores with garden shops, such as those listed here, carry composts and manures and other soil amendments composed, for example, from mushroom litter, chicken or steer manures, and earthworm castings. Also look on their shelves for Ringer and New Life organic fertilizers.

Fred Meyer, Inc.

Payless

G.I. Joe's

WILLAMETTE VALLEY

Zoo Doo is elephant manure scooped straight from the elephant house with nothing added. If you'd like to add this exotic amendment to your soil, call Portland's Washington Park Zoo at 226-1516 and make a reservation to pick it up on Saturday morning between 7:30 and 7:45. The prices are low—$10 a truckload, $8 a small truckload—and zoo staff will help you fill your bin. You can also fill your own garbage bag for $1. (Cans of Zoo Doo are on sale for $3.95 in the Zoo Gift Shop.)

Vollstedt's Green Thumb
410 Pacific Blvd. S.W., Albany, OR 97321
928-2521
Carries the complete Whitney Farms line of both composts and organic fertilizer.

McFarlane's Bark, Inc.
13345 S.E. Johnson Rd., Clackamas, OR 97015
659-4240
Carries mulch made of yard debris in bulk, in fine, medium, and coarse grades. The mulch runs from $3 to $13 for half a pickup load (one and a fourth cubic yards). Contact Theresa McFarlane or John McFarlane.

Garland Nursery
5470 N.E. Hwy. 20, Corvallis, OR 97330
753-6601

Carries the complete Whitney Farms line of organic fertilizer, and a combination of steer and chicken manures and forest humus.

Down to Earth Farm and Garden
Fifth Ave. & Olive St., Eugene, OR 97402
342-6820
Staffed by experts in organic gardening, Down to Earth carries a vast line to rejuvenate your soil organically. This is the gardening retail outlet, just a few blocks away from Down to Earth Distributors, which supplies organic fertilizers for garden shops all over the state.

Gray's Garden Shop
737 W. Sixth Ave., Eugene, OR 97402
345-1569
Both stores carry the Whitney Farms and Webfoot lines, from kelp meal to bat guano. They also sell mushroom compost and all the basic barnyard manures.

444 E. Main St., Springfield, OR 97478
747-2301

Oregon Garden Store
333 S. State St., Lake Oswego, OR 97034
697-3635
Carries Maxicrop, Whitney Farms, and from Down to Earth a seaweed with micronutrients.

Northwoods Nursery
28696 S. Cramer Rd., Molalla, OR 97038
651-3737
Northwoods Nursery is open from the middle of January to the end of October. It carries All Organic Fertilizer (a premixed blend of mineral, animal, and plant fertilizers), greensand, soft rock phosphate, Maxicrop (seaweed powder), and an acid plant mix.

Curt Lafferty's
4435 S.W. Beaverton-Hillsdale Hwy., Portland, OR 97221
246-3722
Carries blended soil (sand, garden mulch, and topsoil) from $15 to $18 per cubic yard. It's sold in bulk, so you'll need a pickup.
Contact Curt Lafferty.

Dennis' 7 Dees
6025 S.E. Powell Blvd., Portland, OR 97206
777-1421
All three garden shops carry a wide variety of organic fertilizers in the Whitney Farms, Ringer, and Down to Earth lines, plus amendments including cottonseed meal and blood meal and greensand, in bulk. Nature's Cycle is an organic lawn and garden fertilizer that adds microorganisms. The garden shops also sell mushroom compost plus steer, chicken, and barnyard manures.

10445 S.W. Barnes Rd., Portland, OR 97225
297-1058

1090 McVey Ave., Lake Oswego, OR 97034
636-4660

Dragonfly Gardens
2230 S.E. Hawthorne Blvd., Portland, OR 97202
235-9150
Besides boxes of organic fertilizer, Dragonfly has bins of bone meal, cottonseed meal, diatomaceous earth, lime, greensand, gypsum, kelp, peat, perlite, rock phosphate, vermiculite, and soils. Scoop what you need into recycled garden sacks to build your soil. It also sells mushroom and Kosher composts; barnyard, steer, and chicken manures.

Drake's 7 Dees
16519 S.E. Stark St., Portland, OR 97233
255-9225
Carries the Whitney Farms and Ringer lines of organic fertilizers, and mushroom and Kosher composts.

Earth Mercantile
6345 S.W. Capitol Hwy., Portland, OR 97201
246-4935
Carries some Whitney Farms and Down to Earth products, plus mushroom compost.

East County Recycling
12409 N.E. San Rafael St., Portland, OR 97230
253-0867

Carries mulch made from the yard debris the recycling center has received. You'll have to haul it with a pickup, but it's free. Contact Ralph Gilbert.

If Not Now...When?
512 N.W. Twenty-first Ave., Portland, OR 97201
222-4471
Carries a variety of composts and manures in the spring and summer.

Kosher
4450 N.E. Buffalo St., Portland, OR 97218
284-4086
For the three years we've been using Kosher we've wondered about the name. It's for Eric Kosher, the company owner, and the compost is made of animal manures and shavings from animal bedding; whatever that is, our garden loves it. You can find Kosher recycled bags of compost in garden shops all over Portland, or go straight to the plant and pay $12 a square yard (delivery charge extra).

Northwest Garden Spot
2635 N.W. Thurman St., Portland, OR 97210
274-2439
Besides carrying the complete Whitney Farms line, this store is one of the few we've found that sells organic fertilizers in bins—and it provides recycled bags for you to haul away soil amendments. Posted over the bins are recipes for mixing compost and fertilizer. It also carries Kosher and mushroom composts, the barnyard composts, and earthworm castings.

Portland Nursery
5050 S.E. Stark St., Portland, OR 97215
231-5050
Carries one of the most complete lines of organic fertilizers. Besides Whitney Farms and Webfoot the nursery offers bulk bags from Down to Earth. It also sells mushroom and Kosher composts, and barnyard, steer, and chicken manures.

Guentner's Gardens
5780 Commercial St. S.E., Salem, OR 97306
585-7133
Carries Ringer lawn fertilizer and the complete Whitney Farms line. It also sells mushroom compost and barnyard manures.

Grimm's Fuel Company
18850 S.W. Cipole Rd., Tualatin, OR 97062
692-3756
Carries hemlock and fir bark mulch for $33 and $31 per pickup load (two and a half cubic yards). Grimm's will deliver four cubic yards of hemlock mulch for $71 and fir mulch for $64. Mushroom mulch runs a little higher. Contact Jeff Grimm.

S and H Logging
20200 S.W. Stafford Rd., Tualatin, OR 97062
638-1011
Carries bark mulch in bulk, made from yard debris, for $15 per cubic yard; mushroom compost for $20 per yard. For $20 extra S and H will deliver. Contact Loretta Stroupe.

SOUTHERN OREGON

Ray's Garden Center
2265 Hwy. 66, Ashland, OR 97520
482-9561
Carries Allegro and Whitney Farms lines of composts and organic fertilizers.

Chet's Garden Center
229 S.W. H St., Grants Pass, OR 97526
476-4424
Carries rose and flower food by Whitney Farms, bone meal, mushroom and redwood composts, and barnyard manures.

Redwood Nursery
1290 Redwood Ave., Grants Pass, OR 97527
476-2642
Carries Webfoot, Whitney Farms, and Down to Earth composts and organic fertilizers.

Radford's Altamont Nursery
3237 Maryland Ave., Klamath Falls, OR 97603
884-0669
Carries the Webfoot and Whitney Farms lines.

EASTERN AND CENTRAL OREGON

Landsystems
21336 Hwy. 20 E., Bend, OR 97701
389-5926

Carries the complete lines of Melorganite organic fertilizer and Desert Bloom organic lawn care, plus mushroom compost and chicken manure.

Redmond's Greenhouse
4101 S. Hwy. 97, Redmond, OR 97756
548-5418

Carries Ringer lawn fertilizer, Down to Earth organic fertilizers, and mushroom compost, fir bark, and steer and chicken manures. On Earth Day Redmond's Greenhouse gave away 250 tree seedlings.

THE COAST

Raintree Garden and Gift
Hamlet Rt. Box 304, Seaside, OR 97138
738-6980

Carries Allegro and Webfoot organic fertilizers, mushroom compost, and various barnyard manures.

MANUFACTURERS AND DISTRIBUTORS:

Bioterra
P.O. Box 431, Independence, OR 97351
838-6001

Bioterra enhances soil enzymatic activity and makes your plants more aromatic. It is approved for organic certified growers and can be found in organic farm and garden stores. For information contact Robin Olsen.

Down to Earth Distributors
850 W. Second Ave., Eugene, OR 97402
485-5932

Down to Earth offers fifteen different organic fertilizers, including steamed bone meal and bat guano. Contact Jack Bates.

Garden Grow
P.O. Box 278, 6500 Hanna Rd., Independence, OR 97351
838-2811

Garden Grow is a distributor of the Whitney Farms line. It offers nine different soil amendments and nine fertilizers. All the products are 100 percent organic.

Inland Pacific Fisheries
P.O. Box 719, Ontario, OR 97914
(800) 752-4887
Inland Pacific Fisheries has fish fertilizer, dormant fish oil for orchards, bone meal, and fish emulsion and kelp. It wholesales and retails. Contact Jim Bashrenburg.

Oregon Organic Supply, Inc.
7566 Perrydale Loop, Amity, OR 97101
(800) 227-8975, (503) 363-1352
Oregon Organic's fertilizers come in bags or bulk and can be custom mixed. It supplies commercial growers and distributors mainly, but is making plans for a retail store in Perrydale next year. Contact Rob Gould.

South Coast Organic Growers Association
P.O. Box 155, Broadbent, OR 97414
572-5564
South Coast Organic Growers is a support group for both organic commercial farmers and home gardeners in Coos and Curry counties. It offers a certification program like Oregon Tilth's, provides workshops, and prints an organic newsletter. Contact Roland Ransdell.

MAIL ORDER:
Bio-Systems
6359 Euclid St., Marlette, MI 48453
(517) 635-2864
Offers a variety of organic amendments for your garden.

Davina Colvin
11171 Charnock Rd. #2, Los Angeles, CA 90034
(213) 397-2757
Mineral-rich rock dust added to soil, along with humus or compost, provides an immediate source of nourishment to healthy and troubled plants. Order it for $1 plus postage for one pound; $20 plus postage for fifty pounds. Call for larger-quantity prices.

Ecology Action
5798 Ridgewood Rd., Willits, CA 95490
(No phone)
Biointensive fertilizers for your biodynamic garden, including a starter

kit, are only $10. Ecology Action also carries foliar sprays and kelp in liquid, meal, and powder form.

EcoSource
9051 Mill Station Rd., Bldg. E, Sebastopol, CA 95472
(800) 688-8345
Wiggle Worm Soil Builder is sold in one-pound ($1.98) and thirty-pound ($14.98) sizes.

Gardener's Supply
128 Intervale Rd., Burlington, VT 05401
(802) 863-1700
In addition to kelp meal, various all-purpose fertilizers, and bat guano, Gardener's Supply sells worm castings (a soil conditioner), and it is one of the rare sources for calcium-rich cricket castings.

Gardens Alive!
Natural Gardening Research Center
Highway 48, Box 149, Sunman, IN 47041
(812) 623-3800
If you want to buy organic plant food that's right for particular plants, check the Gardens Alive! mixtures for vegetables, flowers, and house plants. The line also includes seaweed products and fish emulsion to supplement soil and deter garden pests.

Harmony Farm Supply
P.O. Box 451, Graton, CA 95444
(707) 823-9125
Carries organic soil amendments.

Nichols Garden Nursery
1190 N. Pacific Hwy., Albany, OR 97321
928-9280
Carries Liquid Sea Weed and Bioterra.

Northwoods Nursery
28696 S. Cramer Rd., Molalla, OR 97038
651-3737

Carries All Organic Fertilizer (a premixed blend of mineral, animal, and plant fertilizers), greensand, soft rock phosphate, and Maxicrop (seaweed powder).

Peaceful Valley Farm Supply
P.O. Box 2209, Grass Valley, CA 95945
(916) 272-4769
Carries organic fertilizers and inoculant for soil.

Bargyla Rateaver, Ph.D.
9049 Covina St., San Diego, CA 92126
(619) 566-8994
Dr. Rateaver's products are reasonably priced, and you can get them in small quantities; five-pound bags or larger. She has Maxicrop seaweed powder, which is so soluble it won't cloud your sprayer; seaweed meal that you can use as a foliar spray; and a spray-on enzyme product that replaces enzymes in Maxicrop that are lost in processing. She also has fossil clay, alfalfa meal, bone meal, cottonseed meal, and soybean meal.

Ringer
9959 Valley View Rd., Eden Prairie, MN 55344-3585
(800) 654-1047
Ringer has organic fertilizers specifically blended for acid-loving plants, flower gardens, lawns, indoor plants, berries, and potatoes, tomatoes, and other vegetables.

Territorial Seed Company
P.O. Box 157, Cottage, OR 97424
942-9547
Carries Seaborn Soluble Seaweed, Sunrise Plant Food Tablets (especially good for container gardening), Seaborn 5-10-10, and Organic Fertilizer Mix 4-6-1.

SOIL MOISTURE RETAINER, see WATER CONSERVATION PRODUCTS

SOLAR ENERGY

INFORMATION

STATEWIDE

American Institute Of Architects (AIA)
615 S.W. Park St., Portland, OR 97205
223-8757
The institute can lead you to architects who specialize in solar design.

Consulting Engineers Council Of Oregon
5319 S.W. Westgate Dr., Portland, OR 97221
292-2348
Contact Herb West.

Eugene Water Electric Board (EWEB)
Solar/New Construction Manager
Energy Conservation Center
P.O. Box 10148, Eugene, OR 97440-2148
484-2411
EWEB has a firm commitment to alternative energy sources and gives commercial and residential builders step-by-step help.

Oregon Department of Energy (ODOE)
625 Marion St., Salem, OR 97310
(800) 221-8035, 378-4040
Fax 373-7806
Call and ask for the free *Oregon Solar Energy Directory*. ODOE can answer any questions concerning weatherization and energy tax credits.

Portland General Electric Company
121 S.W. Salmon St., TB6, Portland, OR 97204
691-1726
PGE can offer advice on energy and efficiency.

Professional Engineers of Oregon
1423 S.W. Columbia St., Portland, OR 97201
228-2701
Contact President Steve Hawke.

Solar Energy Association of Oregon
2637 S.W. Water St., Portland, OR 97201

224-7867

Although the association devotes most of its time to theory, planning, and legislative work, Steve Lawrie can direct you to people with information you need.

NATIONWIDE
American Solar Energy Society
2400 Central Ave. #B1, Boulder, CO 80301

A free catalog lists books on solar energy, ranging from home practical advice to theoretical information. The society also publishes a bimonthly magazine on new solar technology.

CAREIRS (Conservation and Renewable Energy Inquiries and Referral Service)
P.O. Box 8900, Silver Spring, MD 20907
(800) 523-2929

Call this service if you want the names of solar energy manufacturers or literature about available solar energy products. It has a nationwide network of contacts and can give you general or highly specific, technical information.

EcoNet
3228 Sacramento St., San Francisco, CA 94115
(415) 923-0900

A computer-based telecommunications network for people worldwide with a PC and modem, EcoNet offers members access to ongoing "conferences" on alternative technologies and conservation (as well as purely theoretical matters). After a $15 sign-up fee, membership is $10 per month.

Hoxan America, Inc.
1 Centennial Plaza, Piscataway, NJ 08854
(800) 344-3546

Offers information on photovoltaic equipment only.

NATAS (National Appropriate Technology Assistance Services)
Department of Energy
P.O. Box 2525, Butte, MT 59702
(800) 428-2525

Call for technical information and for answers to specific questions on solar energy projects. NATAS also has information on home energy conservation and renewable energy sources. If you want to insulate your home or fix a leaking solar panel, it can help.

Solar Energy Industries Association
1730 N. Lynne St. #610, Arlington, VA 22209
(703) 524-6100
The association will refer you to local installers and distributors of solar equipment. It also publishes newsletters on solar energy technologies.

PHOTOVOLTAICS

You can use sunlight to power at least some of your electric needs by converting it into direct current (DC) electricity. For this photovoltaic conversion all you need is solar panels on your roof to become your own power company. Solar electric power is most useful and cost effective for people who live in remote areas not serviced by utility companies. Photovoltaics are being used for recreational vehicles and as an electrical source separate from central power outlets. Many people can furnish at least some of their electrical needs using this nonpolluting power source.

The Oregon companies listed below are dealers certified by the Department of Energy to install solar electric systems. The certification does not imply a guarantee on quality of work.

WILLAMETTE VALLEY
Solar Tech International
16880 S.W. Cynthia St., Aloha, OR 97007
649-3474
Contact Mojo Nwokoma.

Solar Design & Construction
P.O. Box 1241, Corvallis, OR 97339
753-8725
Contact Andy Bortz.

Lane Energy Center
2915 Row River Rd., Cottage Grove, OR 97424
942-0522
Contact Doug Still.

Sun Harvesters/Energia
732 W. Sixth Ave., Eugene, OR 97402
345-3111
Contact Tom Scott.

Renewable Energy, Inc.
1527 N.E. Fifty-first Ave., Portland, OR 97213
287-4777
Contact Don Larson.

Sun, Wind And Fire
7637 S.W. Thirty-third Ave., Portland, OR 97219
254-2661
Contact Brent Gunderson.

Duane's Solar Energy Co.
1625 Cottage St. S.E., Salem, OR 97302
362-9115
Contact Duane Brown.

Free Energy Options
P.O. Box 430, Veneta, OR 97487
935-2749
Contact Leo Morin.

SOUTHERN OREGON

Dependable Power Supply
462 Allison St., Ashland, OR 97520
482-4349
Contact Robert Warren.

Electron Connection
P.O. Box 442, Medford, OR 97501
779-1174
Contact Richard Perez.

Shelter Products N.W.
206 N.E. Jackson St., Roseburg, OR 97470
673-1860
Contact Bill Mann.

MAIL ORDER:

Alternative Energy Engineering
P.O. Box 339 , Redway, CA 95489
(707) 923-2277

Energy Depot
61 Paul Dr., San Rafael, CA 94903
(415) 499-1333

Independent Power Company
P.O. Box 649, North San Juan, CA 95960
(800) 544-6466

Jade Mountain
P.O. Box 4616, Boulder, CO 80306
(303) 449-6601
Carries power generators, solar gate openers, air conditioners, and other equipment. Jade Mountain also publishes newsletters and product information booklets.

Photron, Inc.
149 N. Main St., Willits, CA 95490
(707) 459-3211

Real Goods
966 Mazzoni St., Ukiah, CA 95482
(800) 762-7325
Real Goods has photovoltaic units starting at $149 and doesn't have a vested interest in any manufacturers. If you're technically minded (you can program your own VCR), buy the *Alternative Energy Sourcebook* for $10 and consult its charts and information. Otherwise, call Real Goods for further information. It also has solar outdoor lights for $39 and up. For water heating it sells the Copper Cricket (see the section following on Solar Hot Water and Space Heating, Manufacturer). Real Goods also carries Heliocol solar pool heaters. Since the price varies depending on the size of your pool, call for more information.

Solar Electric Engineering, Inc.
116 Fourth St., Santa Rosa, CA 95401
(707) 542-1990

Fax (707) 542-4358

This company designs and builds solar homes. It offers a wide variety of solar electric generating equipment, the necessary accessories, and low-energy appliances, as well as what you might need for solar water heating. Call for *The Environmental Catalog*, a free products catalog, and ask about *The Solar Electric Book* for $11.95. On September 6, 1990 it also generated the Electric Motor Car Company (EMC2) to produce and market electric vehicles (see under Automobiles and Scooters, Energy Efficient). Solar Electric sells electric car conversion kits and vehicles ranging from electric bicycles to sports cars.

Sunelco
P.O. Box 1499, Hamilton, MT 59840
(406) 363-6924

This photovoltaics company stocks everything from single components, reasonably priced, to fully installed units. It offers a planning guide and catalog for $3.95 that details the design of recreational vehicle, cabin, water-pumping, and total home-power systems.

SOLAR HOT WATER AND SPACE HEATING

Dealers listed here are certified by the Oregon Department of Energy (ODOE); they may install hot water systems without first obtaining a precertification from the ODOE. The certification does not imply a guarantee on quality of work. The dealer you choose will lead you to an installer.

WILLAMETTE VALLEY

Creative Vision Co.
2340 S.W. Fifteenth Ave., Albany, OR 97321
926-5771
Contact Peter Greenburg.

Sundance Solar
4093 W. Eleventh Ave., Eugene, OR 97402
344-1594
Contact Kelly Dancer.

Mr. Sun
68 Touchstone St., Lake Oswego, OR 97034

222-2468
Contact John Patterson.

Sterett Plumbing & Heating
1807 E. Nineteenth St., McMinnville, OR 97128
472-2047
Contact Robert Sterett.

First Street Plumbing Shop
16575 S. Hunter St., Oregon City, OR 97045
656-7463
Contact Wilfred Joe.

Victor Bothe, Solar Broker
4605 S.W. Forty-ninth Ave., Portland, OR 97221
246-4428
Contact Victor Bothe.

Energy Exchange
2806 S.E. Sixty-third Ave., Portland, OR 97202
775-4137
Contact Mike Slover.

Energy Systems N.W.
7421 S.E. Powell Blvd., Portland, OR 97206
777-3370
Contact David Bakke.

Neil Kelly Designers and Remodelers
Energy Division
804 N. Alberta St., Portland, OR 97217
288-2350
Contact Neil Kelly.

Oregon Heat Pump
2200 N.E. Broadway , Portland, OR 97232
228-2350
Contact Dwight Sheldon.

Pride Plumbing & Solar
5614 N.E. Thirtieth Ave., Portland, OR 97211

282-9112
Contact Kip Pinkly.

Renewable Energy, Inc.
1527 N.E. Fifty-first Ave., Portland, OR 97213
287-4777
Contact Don Larson.

Judson Plumbing
1390 Thirteenth St., Salem, OR 97309
363-4141
Contact Tom Jeffries.

Lindsay Softwater Company
18445 S.W. Eighty-sixth St., Tualatin, OR 97062
692-3880

Wolfers, Inc.
290 Young St., Woodburn, OR 97071
981-4511
Contact Robert Love.

SOUTHERN OREGON

Jeff Mackett Plumbing Co.
1801 Siskiyou Blvd., Rm 225, Ashland, OR 97520
488-0382
Contact Jeff Mackett.

Solar Collection
369 Nevada St., Ashland, OR 97520
482-9224
Contact Tim Dawson.

Energyman, Inc.
3946 Lamarada St., Klamath Falls, OR 97603
882-7203
Contact D. C. Long.

Modern Plumbing
317 E. Jackson St., Medford, OR 97501

773-5366
Contact Jack Latvala.

Price Plumbing
40 Belknap Rd., Unit 16, Medford, OR 97501
772-7969
Contact Frank Price.

EASTERN AND CENTRAL OREGON

Bobcat & Sun Construction
65548 Seventy-sixth St., Bend, OR 97701
389-7365
Contact Bob Claridge.

Sunlok of Central Oregon
1225 N.E. Third St., Bend, OR 97708
388-4439
Contact Ron Kiepert.

Mull Tin Shop, Inc.
290 W. Marie St., Hermiston, OR 97838
567-6813
Contact David Mull, Jr.

THE COAST

Miller's Coastal Solar
P.O. Box 1246, Newport, OR 97365
867-7652
Contact George Miller.

MANUFACTURER:

Sage Advance Corp.
1001 Bertelson St., Eugene, OR 97402
485-1947

Listed by *Popular Science* magazine as one of the top 100 products of 1990, the Copper Cricket solar hot water heater circulates an antifreeze solution between a solar collector and a heat exchanger linked to a home's water heater. A passive system, it uses no moving parts and is self-pumping, self-regulating, maintenance-free, and attractive. More than five hundred have been sold, saving approximately one million kilowatt hours of electricity annually. One system can supply all the hot water needs of a four-person household in the summer and a significant percentage during the winter: approximately 50 percent in the Willamette Valley, 60 percent in Southern Oregon, and 70 percent in Eastern Oregon.

Since water heaters account for one quarter of a home energy bill and the Copper Cricket qualifies for an Oregon AED tax credit of $1,172 to $1,470, it easily pays for itself in less than the ten years it's under warranty. The system sells for $2,180 f.o.b. Eugene, Oregon and can be installed by any of the licensed dealers and installers in the state.

TAX CREDITS AND LOANS

Since 1978 Oregon has granted more than fourteen thousand tax credits to help Oregonians pay for energy systems that use renewable sources. This income tax credit for alternative energy devices (AED) covers solar, geothermal, wind, and hydroelectric systems. These systems may be used for water heating, space heating, or electricity production.

The tax credit is based on how much energy the system will save in the first year of use. The more energy saved, the higher the credit, to a limit of $1,500. For most systems the credit is $.60 per kilowatt hour (kWh) of usable energy saved the first year. For pool, spa, and hot tub heating the credit is $.15 per kWh or 50 percent of system cost, whichever is less.

The credit reduces state income taxes owed dollar for dollar; it is not a deduction from taxable income. It can be carried forward for five years if you do not owe enough taxes to claim the entire credit the first year. The tax credit is available for systems purchased between January 1, 1990 and December 31, 1995.

Under Oregon law the value of a solar energy system is exempt from property taxation for assessment years beginning prior to January 1, 1998. For more information call the Oregon Department of Revenue, (800) 371-2244, or Department of Energy (ODOE), (800) 221-8035.

The state of Oregon also operates a loan program through ODOE—the Small Scale Energy Loan Program (S.E.L.P.)—to help pay for most systems. The amount and term of the loan are determined upon application. Funds are obtained by selling Oregon state bonds. Interest rates are low and vary with bond sales. For information call ODOE S.E.L.P, (800) 221-3035 or 373-1033. Most projects funded by S.E.L.P. are also eligible for the state tax credit.

SOLARIZED SHADES, see INSULATION

SPEED BUMPS, *see* **RECYCLED PRODUCTS**

STAINED GLASS, *see* **RECYCLED PRODUCTS**

STRING SHOPPING BAGS, *see* **BAGS, COTTON SHOPPING**

THERMAL GLASS, *see* **INSULATION**

TOPSOIL, *see* **RECYCLED PRODUCTS**

WATER CONSERVATION PRODUCTS..........................

These products make it easy to conserve water. Of what you do use, some portion can be used again; this twenty-six page handbook will help you decide how and where to use gray water in your gardens:

Gray Water Use in the Landscape, by Robert Kourik
Edible Publications: Santa Rosa, 1988. $6, available from:
Edible Publications
P.O. Box 1841, Santa Rosa, CA 95402
(707) 874-2606

CAR WASH ADDITIVE

Water Miser
St. James Industries
P.O. Box 56, Santa Barbara, CA 93102
(805) 963-9400

You can wash and dry your car in fifteen minutes using only one gallon of water when you add this liquid to the water. No hoses, no rinsing. This nonabrasive, nontoxic, silicone-free car-wash solution costs between $2.99 and $3.99 and lasts for sixteen to twenty washes. If you can't find it at your local hardware store, supermarket, automobile supply store, drugstore, or discount store, call the manufacturer for the vendor nearest you. Or call the manufacturer for wholesale orders; you can buy it by the case for $40.80 (twenty-four bottles).

SOIL MOISTURE RETAINER

Most water retainers use plastic polymers, but Sta-Wet uses starch. It can absorb hundreds of times its weight in water and lasts several years. It can be applied directly to the soil or used in pots. The following garden shops have Sta-Wet.

Down to Earth Farm and Garden
Fifth Ave. & Olive St., Eugene, OR 97402
342-6820

Dragonfly Gardens
2230 S.E. Hawthorne Blvd., Portland, OR 97202
235-9150

Earth Mercantile
6345 S.W. Capitol Hwy., Portland, OR 97201
246-4935

Northwest Garden Spot
2635 N.W. Thurman St., Portland, OR 97210
274-2439

DISTRIBUTOR:
Down to Earth Distributors
850 W. Second Ave., Eugene, OR 97402
485-5932

WATERING SYSTEMS AND WATER TIMERS

STATEWIDE
Fred Meyer, Inc.
All Fred Meyer garden shops carry Rain-Drip irrigation systems, water timers, and soaker hoses.

WILLAMETTE VALLEY
Vollstedt's Green Thumb
410 Pacific Blvd. S.W., Albany, OR 97321
928-2521
Carries soaker hoses and water timers.

Garland Nursery
5470 N.E. Hwy. 20, Corvallis, OR 97330
753-6601
Carries drip irrigation systems, soaker hoses, and water timers.

Down to Earth Farm and Garden
Fifth Ave. & Olive St., Eugene, OR 97402
342-6820
Carries equipment for tree irrigation systems, "leaky pipes," and a gauge that tells how much water you need.

Gray's Garden Shop
737 W. Sixth Ave., Eugene, OR 97402
345-1569
Both stores carry drip irrigation systems, soaker hoses, and water timers.

444 E. Main St., Springfield, OR 97478
747-2301

Oregon Garden Store
333 S. State St., Lake Oswego, OR 97034
697-3635
Carries soaker hoses.

Dennis' 7 Dees
6025 S.E. Powell Blvd., Portland, OR 97206
777-1422
All three stores carry drip irrigators, water timers, and soaker hoses. Dave Worthington is the irrigation specialist.

10445 S.W. Barnes Rd., Portland, OR 97225
297-1058

1090 McVey Ave., Lake Oswego, OR 97034
636-4660

Dragonfly Gardens
2230 S.E. Hawthorne Blvd., Portland, OR 97202
235-9150
Carries drip irrigation systems, soaker hoses, and water timers.

Drake's 7 Dees
16519 S.E. Stark St., Portland, OR 97233
255-9225
Carries drip irrigation systems, soaker hoses, and water timers.

Portland Nursery
5050 S.E. Stark St., Portland, OR 97215
231-5050
Carries drip irrigation systems, soaker hoses, and water timers.

Guentner's Gardens
5780 Commercial St. S.E., Salem, OR 97306
585-7133
Carries drip irrigation systems, soaker hoses, and water timers.

SOUTHERN OREGON

Ray's Garden Center
2265 Hwy. 66, Ashland, OR 97520
482-9561
Carries drip irrigation systems, soaker hoses, and water timers.

Chet's Garden Center
229 S.W. H St., Grants Pass, OR 97526
476-4424
Carries Rain-Drip's entire line, soaker hoses, and four types of water timers.

Redwood Nursery
1290 Redwood Ave., Grants Pass, OR 97527
476-2642
Carries drip irrigation systems, soaker hoses, and water timers.

Radford's Altamont Nursery
3237 Maryland Ave., Klamath Falls, OR 97603
884-0669
Carries soaker hoses, and will install water timers.

EASTERN AND CENTRAL OREGON

Landsystems
21336 Hwy. 20 E., Bend, OR 97701
389-5926
Carries low-flow drip systems and water timers.

Redmond's Greenhouse
4101 S. Hwy. 97, Redmond, OR 97756

548-5418
Carries Aqua-Drip irrigation systems, soaker hoses, and one kind of water timer (and can order others).

THE COAST
Raintree Garden and Gift
Hamlet Rt., Box 304, Seaside, OR 97138
738-6980
Carries soaker hoses.

MAIL ORDER:
The Alsto Company
P.O. Box 1267, Galesburg, IL 61401
(800) 447-0048
Sells soaker hoses: 25 feet for $12.50; 50 feet for $17.50.

Gardener's Supply
128 Intervale Rd., Burlington, VT 05401
(802) 863-1700
Gardener's Supply carries the battery-operated Nelson water computer, which is simple to program for as many as three watering periods per day on a seven-day schedule; $49.95.
Hydro-Grow hose is 25 feet for $12.95, 50 feet for $19.95, 100 feet for $37.75, and 250 feet for $79.95. There are also supplies with which to customize your system, and free design service.

Harmony Farm Supply
P.O. Box 451, Graton, CA 95444
(707) 823-9125
Harmony's huge catalog has a complete selection of soaker hoses and drip-irrigation systems for commercial or residential use. It also includes design information.

Nitron
4605 Johnson Rd., Fayetteville, AR 72702
(800) 835-0123
Wet-Flex soaker hose is 25 feet for $12, 50 feet for $19.98, and 100 feet for $34. This is do-it-yourself hose with separate fittings for customizing your system, and it comes with a free system-designing booklet.

Ringer
9959 Valley View Rd., Eden Prairie, MN 55344-3585
(800) 654-1047
Sells a manual two-hour water timer for $26.98; a battery-operated water computer timer is $59.98.

Smith and Hawken
25 Corte Madera, Mill Valley, CA 94941
(415) 383-2000
The Gardena patio drip kit, containing 75 feet of pipe, water emitters and couplings, hose and water-stop connectors, pressure regulator, filter, and more, is $49. Smith and Hawken also carries Root Quencher soaker hoses, separately and in sets with enough fittings to set up five lateral rows; $49.50 and up for a 50-foot set.

WATER RESTRICTORS AND A RECYCLER

Hardware stores
The gizmo that fits on your water faucet to reduce water flow is called a water restrictor. It will turn everyone in your home into a water conserver. You can find a variety of these very common items at most hardware stores.

E.M.A. (Environmental Marketing Association)
P.O. Box 70, Ojai, CA 93024
(805) 646-4647
When you have a color-coordinated bathroom and can't find a low-flow toilet that will match, or you've just gone to considerable expense to install new toilets that are not low flow, there is still a means of cutting back toilets' use of water. For $39.95 E.M.A. offers the Royal Flush, which is easily installed in your current toilet tank and enables you to use as little as one gallon of water per flush.

Solar Electric
116 Fourth St., Santa Rosa, CA 95401
(800) 832-1986, (707) 542-1900
Fax (707) 542-4358
The "Flush-n-Save" converts any toilet to a water saver and can be installed in minutes without tools; $17.95. The "Incredible Superbowl" is a toilet dam device that can save 36 to 42 percent of water consumption; call for price. With a compact tank and pedestal base, "Aqualine" toilets

have smooth lines with a "European look." They use a one and one-half gallon flush, save water at a rate up to 70 percent above industry standards, and cost $175 for white, $245 for a variety of designer colors.

Water Cycle Co.
1038 Redwood Hwy. #1, Mill Valley, CA 94941
(415) 381-7851
The Rinse Recycle System diverts your washing-machine rinse water into a holding tank, from which it's pumped into your drip irrigation system or underground perforated pipe. It costs about $350.

WATERING SYSTEMS, see WATER CONSERVATION PRODUCTS

WATER PURIFIERS AND FILTERS

Wonder how pure your water is and how safe it is to drink? You may want to have it tested before buying a filtration system (look in the Yellow Pages under Environmental Services).

MAIL ORDER:
Nitron Industries, Inc.
4605 Johnson Rd., Fayetteville, AR 72702
(800) 835-0123
Nitron sells the Rainshower dechlorinating unit for showers for $56 and, for the same price, the GardenShower dechlorinating unit for the water you use on your plants. Each unit carries a warranty for one year.

Real Goods
966 Mazzoni St., Ukiah, CA 95482
(800) 762-7325
Real Goods can advise you about the best filtration system for your needs, from countertop to under-the-sink to shower head and travel units. It carries purifiers that use reverse osmosis (making distilled water) and carbon filters; it also sells one that contains a Magnalyte filter, which is the most effective in reducing lead. The prices are low. If you are not on a municipal or pretreated water system, Real Goods will test your water for just $7, then make recommendations. It also sells the Rainshower shower filter to remove chlorine, for $59.

Solar Electric
116 Fourth St., Santa Rosa, CA 95401
(800) 832-1986, (707) 542-1900
Fax (707) 542-4358

Multi-Pure drinking water filter systems remove chemicals like TCE, bacteria, toxic metals, pesticides, and chlorine. Countertop and under-sink models are from $209 to $329. The Instapure Faucet Water Filter is $29.95; the Rainshower dechlorinator, $69.95; the PowerSurvivor desalinizer for sailors, $19.95.

Walnut Acres
Penns Creek, PA 17862
(800) 433-3998

The Bionaire filtration system removes all bacteria and molds and 99.8 percent of trihalomethanes, pesticides, and herbicides. It does not remove fluoride or minerals. Countertop or under-sink models are $249; a replaceable filter is $119.

WATER RESTRICTORS AND A RECYCLER, see WATER CONSERVATION PRODUCTS

WATER TIMERS, see WATER CONSERVATION PRODUCTS

Weatherization

FREE ENERGY AUDITS

Efficient heating and cooling systems, storm doors and windows, weatherstripping, and insulation save energy; they also save money and make your home or apartment more comfortable.

The first step is a free energy audit. The audit does not oblige you to anything. If you heat with oil, call the Oregon Department of Energy's State Home Oil Weatherization (SHOW) program toll free at (800) 452-8660. In Portland call SHOW at 231-7071. If you heat with natural gas or electricity, call your utility. If you heat with wood only, call the utility that heats your water. An appointment will be made for the audit, usually within sixty days. An energy auditor will come to your house or apartment and tell you what you can do to cut your bill and save energy, and can also help you find a qualified contractor.

TAX CREDITS, REBATES, AND LOW-INTEREST LOANS

In Oregon any renter, homeowner, or landlord is eligible for tax credits, cash rebates, and low-interest loans that cut the costs of weatherization and other energy-saving measures. ODOE and your utility can help (see the information numbers at the end of this section). Applications must be approved before work begins. Many cost-reducing programs are available; here is a summary of eligibility groups and the programs designed for them.

If you heat by electricity and your utility is investor owned:
- Low- or no-interest, five to ten-year loans up to $5,000; or
- Twenty-five percent cash rebates for recommended measures up to $350.

If you heat with electricity and your utility is publicly owned, a "POU," that like most POUs, takes part in the Bonneville Power Administration "Buyback" program:
- Cash rebates for recommended measures; as much as 85 percent of the total cost.

If you heat with natural gas:
- Twenty-five percent cash rebate for recommended measures, up to $350; or
- Low-interest, five to ten-year loans up to $5,000.

If you heat with oil, propane, butane, kerosene, or wood, SHOW programs offer:
- Six and a half percent loans to finance weatherization, with no income limit. These are offered through private lenders; call ODOE (see below) for a lender list.
- Cash rebates for up to 50 percent of the cost of weatherization, up to $1,000. These are limited to moderate-income owners and renters; for example, the income limit for a family of four is $31,845.

If you use any fuel type in a low-income home:
- Free weatherization. Income limits depend on family size; for example, in a single-person household your yearly income cannot exceed $7,474. An extra $2,675 is allowed for each additional household member. ODOE (see listing below) can tell you what agency in your community offers this program.

If you own rental property:
- A 35 percent tax credit for energy-saving measures can be taken over five years.
- Most projects must save 10 percent or more of the current energy expenditure and they must be approved before any work is done.

If you are a homeowner:
- Alternative Energy Device (AED) tax credits of up to $1,500 can be taken for the installation of alternative energy systems. (See the Solar Energy section on Tax Credits and Loans.)

Any questions about weatherization programs can be referred to:
Community Energy Project
P.O. Box 12272, Portland, OR 97212
284-6827
If you live in Portland and have a low to moderate income, you are eligible to take one of the Community Energy Project's workshops on how to weatherize your home and cut energy costs. Thirty workshops are scheduled in the fall and early winter; they fill up fast, so sign up early.

Oregon Department of Energy (ODOE)
625 Marion St. N.E., Salem, OR 97310
(800) 221-8035
Salem 378-4040

Portland Energy Conservation, Inc.
921 S.W. Washington St., Ste. 840, Portland, OR 97214
248-4636
PECI offers information about energy programs and also technical assistance.

State Home Oil Weatherization (SHOW) Program
P.O. Box 42227, Portland, OR 97242
(800) 452-8660
Portland 231-7071

WEATHERSTRIPPING, see INSULATION

WINDOW FILM, see INSULATION

Wind Power

The wind can pump water, produce electricity, and provide mechanical energy for a number of tasks. Before you buy any of the equipment required, be sure you measure your wind resource. For more information check with Oregon State University and the Oregon Department of Energy (ODOE). Not all sections of the state have wind consultants or electric system dealers, but their numbers are increasing; this list may be incomplete, and no endorsements are intended. Wind devices are eligible for the Oregon AED tax rebate (see the Solar Energy section on Tax Credits and Loans, for more information).

CONSULTANTS

WILLAMETTE VALLEY

Marias International
1110 N.W. Thirty-fifth St., Corvallis, OR 97330
753-0927

Pacific Wind Energy
Box 1671, Corvallis, OR 97339
753-3139

SOUTHERN OREGON

Foehn Consulting
P.O. Box 5123, Klamath Falls, OR 97601
884-3023

NATIONWIDE

R. Lynette & Associates
7353 148th Ave. N.E., Redmond, WA 98052
(206) 885-0206

WIND ELECTRIC SYSTEM DEALERS

EASTERN AND CENTRAL OREGON

Gorge Wind Electric Power
1550 State Rd., Mosier, OR 97040
478-3363

THE COAST
Baughman & Son
P.O. Box 270, Coos Bay, OR 97420
267-6754

WATER PUMPING WINDMILL DEALERS
WILLAMETTE VALLEY
Aeromotor
16750 S.W. Seventy-second Ave., Portland, OR 97224
620-7964

SOUTHERN OREGON
Chuck's Pump Service
1315 Beekman, Medford, OR 97501
779-4651

EASTERN AND CENTRAL OREGON
Searing Electric & Plumbing
1259 E. Second St., Bend, OR 97701
389-4618

Newton Pump
1921 N. Sixth St., Redmond, OR 97756
548-3502

THE COAST
Perry Electric & Plumbing
3133 Broadway St., North Bend, OR 97459
756-2051

WINDOW TINTING, see INSULATION
YARD DEBRIS, see RECYCLING

TO BE LISTED IN FUTURE DIRECTORIES, please make a copy of this form, fill it out completely, and mail to: The Save Directories, 925 SE Tacoma St., Portland, OR 97202. Use a separate form for each category you would like us to list you under.

CATEGORY _____

NAME OF BUSINESS _____

ADDRESS _____

CITY _____ STATE _____ ZIP _____

PHONE _____

PERSON TO CONTACT _____

NAME OF PRODUCT OR SERVICE _____

DESCRIPTION _____

_____

_____

_____

COST _____

....

DO NOT FILL IN. FOR OFFICE USE ONLY.

DATE REC'D _____

ACCEPTED _____ REJECTED _____

REASONS: _____

_____